IDORA PARK

The Last Ride of Summer

by Rick Shale and Charles J. Jacques, Jr.
designed by Karen Morrison

AMUSEMENT PARK JOURNAL

P.O. Box 478 Jefferson, OH 44047-0478
(440) 576-6531   Fax: (440) 576-5850
E-mail: apjacqu@suite224.net

DEDICATION

This book is dedicated with love to my wife, Betty Van Pelt Jacques.

CHARLES J. JACQUES, JR.

In memory of Alan L. Leach (1947-1987).

RICK SHALE

THE AUTHORS

RICK SHALE was born and raised in the Youngstown area and is a graduate of Boardman High School. He earned a Bachelor of Arts degree from Ohio Wesleyan University and Master of Arts and Ph.D. degrees in American Culture from the University of Michigan.

Shale is a Professor of English and American Studies at Youngstown State University, Youngstown, Ohio, where he teaches courses in film study. He is the author of several articles on film and popular culture. His previous books include *Donald Duck Joins Up: The Walt Disney Studio During World War II* and three books on the Academy Awards, including *The Academy Awards Index: The Complete Categorical and Chronological Record.*

Shale resides in Boardman, Ohio.

CHARLES J. JACQUES, JR. was born and raised in Natrona Heights, Pennsylvania. After attending public schools there, he received a Bachelor of Science degree from the Pennsylvania State University majoring in history. He received a Juris Doctor degree from the University of Pittsburgh's law school in 1965. Jacques resides in Jefferson, Ohio.

Jacques has written four prior books and numerous historical articles on amusement park subjects. He was one of the charter members of the American Coaster Enthusiasts and a past president of the National Carousel Association. Jacques' previous books include *Kennywood: Roller Coaster Capital of the World; Goodbye, West View Park, Goodbye; Hersheypark: The Sweetness of Success;* and *More Kennywood Memories.*

PHOTOGRAPH CREDIT:
Cover: Richard Munch

Copyright © 1999 Charles J. Jacques, Jr.

All rights reserved. No part of this book may be used or reproduced in any manner whatsoever without written permission except in the case of brief quotations embodied in critical articles and reviews. Printed in the United States of America. For information write to Amusement Park Journal, P.O. Box 478, Jefferson, OH 44047.

ISBN # 0-9614392-6-2

Library of Congress Catalog Card Number 99-072061

TABLE OF CONTENTS

1	The Fire		2
2	A Trolley Park for Youngstown	1899 - 1909	6
3	A New Era	1910 - 1920	22
4	Billings Takes Charge	1921 - 1930	38
5	The Big Band Years	1931 - 1945	56
6	The Post-War Period	1946 - 1954	76
7	The Baby Boom	1955 - 1959	86
8	Competition Heats Up	1960 - 1970	94
9	Searching for a Strategy	1971 - 1980	102
10	Going Downhill Fast	1981 - 1984	110
	Appendices		129
	Selected Bibliography		136
	Acknowledgments		138
	Index		139

1st Printing August, 1999
2nd Printing July, 2000

1 THE FIRE

In the last week of April 1984 the management of Idora Park, Youngstown, Ohio, happily welcomed a shift in the temperature that signaled the arrival of summer. The cold, blustery weather that produced a wind chill factor of twenty degrees earlier in the week had ended, and the rain had given way to sunshine. Temperatures rose to the high 60s and 70s, a blessing for the park's workers at Idora Park who were busy preparing for Idora's opening in ten days.

One of the jobs on the schedule for Thursday, April 26th, was to repair the metal channel of the Lost River ride. Shortly before noon, when most of the workers were on lunch break, Pat Duffy, Jr., president and general manager of the Idora Amusement Company, looked out the back window of the park office and saw smoke. A spark from a welder's torch had ignited part of the Lost River ride's wooden supports that held the metal channel. Duffy and some of his employ-

Fire engulfs the midway.
© THE VINDICATOR, 1999

Aerial view looking south toward the fire scene.
© The Vindicator, 1999

The south end of the Wildcat roller coaster was soon in flames.
© The Vindicator, 1999

ees first attempted to fight the blaze with hand-held extinguishers, but the fire quickly roared out of control. An alarm was phoned in, and firefighters were notified of an emergency that would have a lasting effect on the people of Youngstown and the surrounding communities: Idora Park was on fire!

The first firefighters on the scene were hampered by a swirling wind and low water pressure in the park's only operating fire hydrant. A second hydrant was so old that it had been shut off. The flames quickly spread from the Lost River ride to the park office and then to the Wildcat roller coaster. Park employees scrambled to save the office records. Some current files were carried to safety, but the older files and historical records were lost to the flames.

Quick action by firefighters saved the carousel.
© THE VINDICATOR, 1999

Most of the lower midway was destroyed.
© THE VINDICATOR, 1999

A hose relay was quickly set up to hydrants located outside the park on Rogers Road and Parkview Avenue, and an aerial truck began spraying down the park's carousel building in order to save the historic 1922 merry-go-round. In less than an hour, the fire destroyed the Lost River ride, the park office, many game and refreshment stands on the midway, and the second hill and south turn of the Wildcat coaster. Nearly fifty firefighters, including a dozen who were off-duty and working without pay, finally controlled the blaze and kept it from spreading to other parts of the park.

Headlines in the Youngstown *Vindicator* that evening read "Idora Coaster Fire Spreads, Fight To Save Rest of Park," and shock waves went through the community. The following evening's headlines were more optimistic: "Idora Will Try To Open Despite $2.5 Million Fire." Park president Pat Duffy, Jr. vowed to open the park on schedule, despite the damage.

On the day of the fire, the American Coaster Enthusiasts were holding their annual spring meeting at Kings Island near Cincinnati. When news of the fire and the Wildcat's loss was announced at the meeting, there were gasps. Everyone hoped that the Wildcat could be repaired. More than fifty members of the coaster group stopped at Idora on their way home to see the damage for themselves.

Idora's owners moved swiftly to counter the effects of the fire. A temporary office was set up, and the midway was quickly rebuilt with temporary trailers. But Idora's premiere attractions, the Wildcat and the Lost River ride, were so badly damaged that the park could not afford to salvage them. The Idora Amusement Company, the owner of Idora Park, simply did not have the resources needed to reconstruct the coaster, which ranked as one of the best in the country.

Idora Park opened on schedule on May 5th and operated for the full 1984 season, but attendance, which was already in decline, fell even further. By summer's end the inevitable had to be faced: the park would cease operation. For the first time in eighty-five years Youngstowners faced the grim prospect of a summer without Idora Park. As the end of the season approached, visitors, perhaps motivated by nostalgia or a sense of history, flocked to the park to take the last ride of summer.

Firefighters continued to hose down the smoldering ruins.
PHOTOGRAPH BY BOB FULLERMAN

The south end of the Wildcat was destroyed.
PHOTOGRAPH BY BOB FULLERMAN

1899 - 1909

2 A TROLLEY PARK FOR YOUNGSTOWN

Idora Park, like most early amusement parks, could trace its origins to the popularity of fairs and expositions that swept America during the last years of the nineteenth century. Street railway companies found in this thirst for popular amusements a way to increase ridership in the evenings and on the weekends when the regular commuter traffic slacked off: they began to build pleasure grounds. These parks were usually built at the end of the trolley line and thus were called terminal parks. They generally contained some rides and concessions, and they proved immediately popular. The spread of the street railway system and the low fares—generally a nickel—enabled townspeople, especially women and children, to travel conveniently and inexpensively outside the city limits.

Horse-drawn streetcar service began in Youngstown in 1874, and the first electric streetcars appeared in 1890 or 1891. America was becoming electrified, and in the next decade nearly a dozen traction companies sprang up in the Youngstown area. In 1893 the Youngstown Park & Falls Street Railway Company, the developer of Idora Park, was incorporated, though it did not actually begin operation until 1897. The trolley company was named for its original intended destination—Mill Creek Park and Lanterman's Falls—although the line was never extended into Mill Creek Park. However, a persistent rumor circulates that the trolley line was named for two men. A Willis H. Park was on the board of directors by 1899, but neither he nor any Mr. Falls was listed among the trolley company's original founders.

In April 1894 the Park & Falls Street Railway Company petitioned the county commissioners for a franchise to operate a line south of the city from Hillman Street to Mill Creek Park. This initial request was opposed by the established traction companies and was refused, apparently on the grounds that the county had no jurisdiction over one of the streets on the proposed route. Harry G. Hamilton, one of the company directors, continued to fight the political and legal battles. By mid-March 1897 the trolley company secured permission, and the Park & Falls Street Railway Company began operation with one car and one employee. The streetcar line would have a considerable effect on the economic growth of Youngstown's south side, but before this could happen two things were necessary: a way to connect the service to Youngstown's Central Square and an attraction to lure people to the end of the line.

In 1897 the Market Street viaduct had not yet been built and people travel-

Lanterman's Falls in Mill Creek Park was once known as Idora Falls and Mill.
MAHONING VALLEY HISTORICAL SOCIETY

ing south from Youngstown had to cross railroad tracks and the Mahoning River by means of a small bridge that had been built at the river level. Travelers then had to negotiate the steep wooded bluffs just south of the river known as Pine Hill and unofficially as Impassable Ridge. "Cars ran for about a year before the Market Street viaduct was built," said Hamilton. "The viaduct was another big fight. . . . When the proposition came up to build a bridge costing $250,000 it was bitterly opposed, both in town and in the country outside. Big interests claimed it would hurt them, and farmers didn't want to be taxed for Youngstown's benefit." The bridge proponents eventually prevailed, and the Market Street viaduct opened on May 22, 1899. For the first time townspeople could travel south from Youngstown's main square without concern for the railroad yards, river, and steep hill that had discouraged previous travelers. The street railway company advertised the safety of the new route, reminding riders that by taking the new bridge they would avoid "all dangers of crossing the many railroad tracks, which are frequently so fatal to passengers."

The Park & Falls directors had determined that an amusement park would attract riders to Youngstown's relatively undeveloped south side, and so they acquired a lease on a seven-acre plot of land adjacent to Mill Creek Park. The property, part of the old William Smith farm, belonged to Col. Lemuel T. Foster (who gave his name to the Fosterville area on Youngstown's south side), a prominent citizen who had surveyed and platted the land in 1894 and had joined the Board of Directors of the Park & Falls Street Railway Company. By 1899 Foster was no longer on the board, but he would hold title to the Idora property until his death in 1911.

The new Market Street viaduct opened a week before the park in 1899.
© THE VINDICATOR, 1999

Col. Lemuel T. Foster owned the land on which Idora was built.
MAHONING VALLEY HISTORICAL SOCIETY

1899 - 1909

Passengers disembark for a day at Idora circa 1904.
MAHONING VALLEY HISTORICAL SOCIETY

Idora was not the first amusement park in the Youngstown area. The Mahoning Valley Railway Company, which operated streetcar lines in Youngstown and an interurban line to Warren, opened Squaw Creek Park near Girard, Ohio, on July 3, 1897. Despite some large crowds, this park went into receivership within six weeks. However, it remained open and by 1902 was operating under the name Ferncliffe Park. After another period of receivership the park opened under new management in April 1903, this time with the name Avon Park.

Avon Park would continue to experience financial difficulties and declined after 1904. A major flood in 1913 destroyed many of the structures, and it closed for good in the mid 1920s. (The present-day Avon Oaks ballroom is the sole remaining evidence of this early trolley park.) As the only trolley park in the Youngstown area, Avon Park must have served as a useful example to the Park & Falls directors when they were making plans for the creation of Idora.

On January 31, 1899, Charles Dahlinger, secretary-treasurer of the Park & Falls Street Railway Company, wrote to Mill Creek Park commissioners Volney Rogers, Henry Tod, and Hamilton Harris and proposed to develop the property into "a pleasure resort or park and erect a casino, dining room, summer theater, merry-go-round, public comfort buildings, etc." The necessary approval was secured, and by spring the company had erected several buildings. Newspapermen were given a tour on May 27th, and the new park opened to the public on Decoration Day, May 30, 1899. Since the new resort was at the terminus of the streetcar line, it was called Terminal Park, though that name was apparently a temporary one since plans for a name contest were soon announced. The Terminal Park was about three and a half miles or a fifteen-minute ride from the center of Youngstown where the line connected with six different railroads: the Pennsylvania, Pittsburg & Western, New York, Lake Erie & Western, Lake Shore and Michigan Southern, and the Pittsburg and Lake Erie. (From 1890 to 1910 the U.S. Post Office spelled Pittsburg without the "h." Some businesses dropped the "h," and some did not.) As the years passed, such accessibility to other towns and states via railroad and interurban lines would become increasingly important, for Idora Park would draw much

Idora's Casino Theater audience originally sat outdoors.
RICK SHALE COLLECTION

Harry G. Hamilton.
MAHONING VALLEY HISTORICAL SOCIETY

Willis H. Park.
MAHONING VALLEY HISTORICAL SOCIETY

Park & Falls streetcars in downtown Youngstown.
MAHONING VALLEY HISTORICAL SOCIETY

business from eastern Ohio and western Pennsylvania.

The Park & Falls superintendent, Robert T. Ivory, was from the Pittsburgh area, as were five of the company's seven directors. Ivory moved to Youngstown to oversee the daily operations of the trolley line. Though only thirty-three years old in 1899, he had thirteen years' experience in constructing street railways and had supervised work in many parts of the country. To manage the park itself, the company called on Edward Stanley, an entertainer and showman who had been born in England. Stanley had come to Youngstown from Cincinnati in 1891. Soon after his arrival he founded and began operating the Globe Museum and Family Theater, located on West Federal Street where the Paramount Theater was later built. Stanley managed Idora for several seasons, and his good reputation with show people helped assure the success of Idora's Casino Theater.

The seven directors of the streetcar company were businessmen who possessed considerable political clout. Harry G. Hamilton of Youngstown was the only one of the original incorporating directors still on the board. He was joined in 1899 by another Youngstowner Willis H. Park. Hamilton and Park were partners in a number of ventures ranging from hotels and public entertainment to lumber and real estate. The remaining five directors hailed from Allegheny, Pennsylvania, a thriving city located across the Allegheny River from Pittsburgh. Joseph Hastings was a contractor who specialized in paving and curbing streets. Robert McAfee was Director of the Department of Public Works (and later Pennsylvania's Secretary of State), and John R. Murphy was Director of the Department of Public Safety in Allegheny. Charles Dahlinger, who served as secretary-treasurer of the Park & Falls line, was an Allegheny attorney. Serving as president of the Park

1899 - 1909

MILL CREEK PARK!

Thursday Night
ST. JOHN'S EPISCOPAL
CHOIR, 45 voices.........
FREE.

Friday Night
DANCING,
Mahoning Orchestra.

PARK & FALLS STREET CARS.

Balloting...
POPULAR SCHOOL TEACHER....
Deposit your votes in the Merry-Go-Round.

& Falls Street Railway Company was Samuel Grier, who had held several political offices in Allegheny County including water assessor, chief clerk in the office of the county clerk of courts, and delinquent tax collector. He was a bank director and president of a plate glass company, a water company, and a coal company.

For that initial season of 1899, the street railway company constructed, as promised, a casino, theater, band stand, swings, drinking fountains, picnic tables, and toilet facilities. An electric merry-go-round with wooden animals carved by Gustav Dentzel of Philadelphia was a major attraction. This first Dentzel carousel featured a menagerie of stationary animals. (A dozen years later a second Dentzel carousel with jumpers would be installed.)

Musical entertainment of all kinds was popular, and a look at the programs on the Casino stage that first month shows the wide range of selections: on June 29th, 1899, a choir from St. John's Episcopal Church presented a free concert. The following night offered dancing with music provided by the Mahoning Orchestra. The Youngstown Military Band under the direction of Professor O.R. Farrar gave two concerts of sacred music on Sunday July 2nd, and the Casino Theater's vaudeville season opened July 3rd with the Seville Sisters, billed as "fancy contortion and transformation dancers," as the headline act. Admission was 5 cents and 10 cents, and entertainment was changed weekly. Matinees were held each afternoon at 3 p. m.; evening shows began at 7:30 sharp.

The park quickly became a favorite gathering place as indicated in a *Vindicator* article describing Fourth of July activities that first season: "From early afternoon until late at night the streetcars were jammed with passengers going to the park and to the theater, merry-go-round, dancing hall; all were crowded to their utmost capacity and thousands sat around under the big trees and enjoyed

Park & Falls streetcar crossing the Market Street viaduct.
RICK SHALE COLLECTION

seeing others enjoy the day."

Streetcars were redefining the concepts of urban space and social mores. The journey on the trolley could sometimes be as interesting as the destination. As David Nye points out in *Electrifying America: Social Meanings of a New America*, "the streetcar's interior made possible a new intimacy with strangers who could be by turns attractive, disconcerting, or disgusting. The interior of the car was a region of possible flirtations, kindnesses, chance encounters, dangers and inconveniences; it was far less predictable than the experience of riding in a railroad train or an automobile. In the small dramas of the streetcar, entrances and exits were the main events, with the conductor and the driver acting as gatekeepers who orchestrated, but did not always control the performance."

Passengers on the Park & Falls line could purchase twenty-seven tickets for $1.00, a price guaranteed when the directors made a bid for the franchise. At less than a nickel a ride, the Park & Falls streetcar was affordable and on some occasions even full of unexpected excitement. The June 30, 1899, *Vindicator* carried an account of a large crowd at the park and noted the following incident: "A heavily loaded trailer jumped the track at the car barns. This necessitated the transferring of passengers and caused some delay in getting the pleasure seekers back to the city. The car was loaded with ladies when it jumped the track and although it bumped over the ties for some distance not a passenger left a seat or uttered a scream. The courage of the ladies caused favorable comment."

So many people were flocking to the park that the directors decided to increase or expand the facilities. The north end of the dancing pavilion had been used to serve refreshments, but this was proving inadequate to handle the demand. A new refreshment building was ordered, as were booths to house additional amusements. These game booths were leased to individual concessionaires, but the Park & Falls Street Railway built the structures to insure a uniform design throughout the park. Willis H. Park an-

The first dancing pavilion, built in 1899, later became Heidelberg Gardens.
MAHONING VALLEY HISTORICAL SOCIETY

nounced that "entertaining features of all kinds that come within the bounds of the legitimate" would be installed. Among these attractions was a pair of black bears that arrived near the end of the summer.

Under the direction of Edward Stanley a new proscenium was built for the Casino Theater, and a drop curtain and additional scenery ordered. The audience sat outdoors under the trees on a hillside. A fence limited access to those who had paid the theater admission. The directors also promised to construct a roller coaster in the near future. A site in the southwest corner of the park was designated for this purpose. Though this coaster would not be built for three more years, the announcement signaled that the directors were committed to making Terminal Park into a ride park.

The success of the trolley line and the amusement park led rather quickly to another business venture by a pair of the Park & Falls directors. Willis H. Park and Harry G. Hamilton, the two Youngstowners on the Park & Falls board, sensed the growing value of the land along the trolley line. Park had already formed his own real estate company and had developed and had given his name to Willis Avenue, which the *Vindicator* called the Fifth Avenue of the south side. In July 1899 Park, Hamilton, and several other local businessmen formed the South Side Land & Improvement

The bear cage at Idora.
COURTESY OF HISTORIC IMAGES

11

1899 - 1909

Idora Park band stand.
RICK SHALE COLLECTION

Company. They purchased 106 acres along the Park & Falls line and announced plans to develop the property into residential lots. One of their main selling points was that the lots were away from the smoke and dirt of Youngstown's mills. Park and Hamilton then formed a lumber company to furnish the materials needed to construct these new homes. With such interrelated enterprises, these men prospered, and Youngstown's south side rapidly developed.

Streetcars left Youngstown's Central Square, or the Diamond as the square was often called at the turn of the century, and traveled south on Market Street to Warren Avenue where the route turned right and followed Warren west to Hillman Street. The line then ran south on Hillman, cut over Grace Avenue (later renamed Sherwood) to Glenwood, turned south on Glenwood and then west on Parkview Avenue to the park.

The cars carried a two-man crew consisting of a uniformed conductor and a motorman. On August 1, 1899, twenty of these employees met and organized a union, forming Youngstown Division 114 of the Amalgamated Association of Street Railway Employees of America. Their newly elected president stressed that the men had no grievances whatsoever with the company. "We are perfectly satisfied," he told reporters. "Our men are getting higher wages than ever paid for similar work here." The wage he spoke of appreciatively was eighteen cents an hour. The Park & Falls line was the first in Youngstown to be unionized, a point that the company publicized in its Labor Day advertising for the Terminal Park, even though the directors had not yet ratified the contract. In a dozen years all streetcar lines in the area would be controlled by the same company, but even after this merger the Park & Falls men retained their own union local. They could not work the other routes, and vice-versa, even though the streetcars by then pulled out of the same car barns.

On August 27, 1899, the largest crowd yet came to the park. The *Vindicator* estimated that 20,000 people spent part of that Sunday at Terminal Park, a remarkable figure even if inflated by the park since Youngstown's population at the time was only 45,000.

Such crowds strained the capacity of the trolley company, and at the September directors' meeting several more improvements were approved. The line was to be double-tracked, and eight more cars were ordered to bring the total to twenty. The directors also approved the union agreement and agreed to enlarge the park's dining hall to accommodate a bowling alley and shooting gallery.

Terminal Park concluded its first season on October 1st with a free concert by the British Grenadier Band led by Lt. Dan Godfrey, said to be the world's greatest bandmaster. The concert was held in the theater, which consisted of a stage that faced away from the midway and open-air seating on the hillside. For this free concert the fence surrounding the theater was removed to accommodate the huge crowd. Two completely different programs were presented, one in the afternoon and one in the evening. The selections included several marches; works by Handel, Wagner, Bizet, and others; and for the finale a "Nautical Fantasie" that concluded with "Rule Brittania" and "The Star-Spangled Banner." At the request of Ed Stanley, Godfrey's band included in their program "The Youngstown Military Band," a new

Park & Falls street railway employees.
© THE VINDICATOR, 1999

Streetcars and horses shared the Market Street viaduct.
RICK SHALE COLLECTION

march composed by Professor O.R. Farrar. Attendance records were broken, and the park concluded its initial season on a successful note.

The streetcar company's next task was to adopt a new name for Terminal Park. A contest for the city's most popular schoolteacher had begun in June, and schoolchildren were encouraged to vote for their favorite teacher every time they rode the streetcar. Fifty dollars in gold would go to the winning teacher with $30 and $20 going to those who placed second and third. The three most popular teachers, in conjunction with the Mill Creek Park commissioners and the Park & Falls management, would select a permanent name for the park.

Interest in voting lagged during summer vacation, and the contest was nearly abandoned. But by mid-September the voting was reestablished, and conductors were supplied with ballots. Students cast their votes in the ballot box located at the merry-go-round building. The winner with 1,834 votes was Emily Gettins, who had recently been appointed supervisor of penmanship and bookkeeping. Jessie Coulter of Fosterville School came in second with 1,711, and Anna Noll of Wood Street School finished third with 856 votes. The $50 prize was no doubt appreciated by Emily Gettins, whose teaching salary for the entire year was only $500. The *Vindicator* noted that many suggested names had been sent in, among them Union, Dewey, Jackson, McKinley, and Greenlawn.

Some sentiment was expressed for naming the park after Harry G. Hamilton. In mid-August the *Vindicator* quoted an anonymous park patron who praised the park and said, "Harry Hamilton, who has labored four years to

A roof and canvas walls were soon added to the theater.
MAHONING VALLEY HISTORICAL SOCIETY

1899 - 1909

A souvenir booklet.
RICK SHALE COLLECTION

Idora Ann Hively, born in 1857. Was the park named for her?
DORIS BECK COLLECTION

get this Park & Falls franchise, and who also suggested a park at the terminal, deserves great credit for this enterprise. I think the teachers should name the park after Mr. Hamilton. He made it possible for the resort to be a reality, and he has labored hard to make it a success. In all fairness, call the place Hamilton Park." A few days later Manager Stanley added his support to the suggestion and asked for a show of hands from the theater audience. "The response must have been very pleasing to the friends of Mr. Hamilton," reported the *Vindicator*, "for nearly, if not every hand in the audience went into the air without any hesitancy." Had the schoolteachers accepted this suggestion, there would have been no mystery surrounding the park's name, but Hamilton Park was not the name chosen.

The park's new name was to be made public on October 7th, but the illness of Park & Falls president Samuel Grier pushed the announcement back. Additional delays prompted officials to consider pushing back the christening ceremony until the following spring. Then, after the name contest seemed to have been almost forgotten, the following small paragraph appeared in the *Vindicator* on November 25, 1899: "Today it was decided to call the terminal park 'Idora Park.' The name was selected and recommended by Miss Jessie Coulter, who teaches in Fosterville and lives in Haselton. She was the second most popular teacher in the contest some time ago, and was awarded a prize of $30. The name Idora is said to be Indian and was the original name of Lanterman's Falls."

As time passed, the confusion over Idora's name grew. On November 27, 1901, the *Youngstown Telegram* called Idora "A Mecca for Youngstown people during the warm summer days and sultry evenings" and gave Emily Gettins credit for naming the park. "The name," stated the article, "is taken from a camp of Indians who made it their home for years."

The word itself has spawned many theories. In an early press release the street railway company said the park was called Idora "after an extinct tribe of Indians which once dwelt within its borders." The park's 1900 souvenir booklet carried a picture of Pioneer Pavilion in Mill Creek Park, identifying it as "the site of Idora Indian village." However, there is no record of any tribe in eastern Ohio called Idora. Their presence in the area and any link to the park remain undocumented.

Idora may indeed be an Indian word, but if so, from what tribe's language does it spring and what does the word mean? More easily corroborated is a possible connection to Lanterman's Falls, located in Mill Creek Park only a few hundred yards from Idora. On this site in 1845 German Lanterman had built and operated a flouring mill. An 1874 atlas identifies Lanterman's Falls as Idora Falls, and a *Vindicator* article in 1896 refers to Idora Falls. The park company's souvenir booklets for years carried a picture captioned Idora Mill and Falls. From such evidence, it would seem that whoever suggested the name may have had the falls in mind.

A widely repeated though uncorroborated story is that Idora is a contraction of "I adore a park." This theory has appeared in print many times, but there is no evidence that it was used when the park's name was selected. Others claim it is a woman's name. A girl named Idora Ann Hively was born in the area in 1857. Her father, Peter Hively, ran a pottery on

Mill Creek about three miles upstream from Idora's location. But this child's connection to the park or the falls is unknown, and she apparently left the area long before Idora Park was named. If Idora Park was named for Idora Falls, then who named the falls? One can only speculate. Another amusement park called Idora Park existed from 1903 to 1929 in Oakland, California. The origins of its name are also uncertain; one possibility is that was named after Youngstown's Idora.

In 1900, the park's second season of operation, the crowds of pleasure seekers going to Idora were greater than ever. The public response to Idora Park as well as the real estate along the line's right of way made the Park & Falls Street Railway Company an attractive business investment in this period of frequent corporate mergers and consolidations. The Mahoning Valley Street Railway, which served the Youngstown area north of the Mahoning River, expressed interest in merging, but the Park & Falls president Samuel Grier rebuffed the offer saying the line was not for sale. Instead, the company decided to put its profits into the park. The vaudeville attractions had been a big draw during the first season, so the theater's outdoor seating was improved. A center aisle was removed, and six hundred new seats were added. Several trees were removed from the hillside to permit a better view of the stage. In addition to the live entertainment, the theater sometimes showed motion pictures using Edison's Projectoscope.

High divers, trapeze artists, and balloon ascensions were some of the attractions that park patrons could see for free at Idora. In August Mademoiselle Alice Zeno drew large crowds to watch her twice daily ascend in a balloon to 3,500 feet and then make a parachute jump.

To remain competitive, the park needed to expand. The *Vindicator* observed, "There is not much doubt but that something will have to be done next season toward having additional attractions at the park...." The creation of a three-and-a-half-acre artificial lake was proposed, but nothing came of it.

No fence enclosed Idora Park, and no admission was charged to enter the grounds. A fee was charged for dancing or the theater or for tickets to the various rides and games, but visitors who wished only to walk through the park or have a picnic could do so for no more than the price of a trolley ride.

Some people, however, were denied access to certain park activities. After having been refused entrance to the dancing pavilion on several occasions, an African-American man filed suit against the park. He lost the case when the Court of Common Pleas ruled that the dancing pavilion was "not a place of public resort under the provisions of the statute." The *Vindicator* reported that the park would be quite pleased with the decision, for "they will now be more particular than ever in the matter of admitting objectionable persons upon the dance floor." The decision, which was extremely discriminatory, reflected the social prejudices of the time.

July 4, 1901, brought crowds to the park to see the fireworks display. The program for the Fourth included the usual bomb shells and rockets as well as a 5-foot bust of Washington, a 20-foot Tree of Hope, a Grand Illumination, and revolving wheels in different colors. The show was a great success, and Idora enjoyed a record-breaking crowd estimated at thirty thousand.

Two weeks later the directors

A souvenir from Idora's photo studio.
EDWARD C. LEARNER COLLECTION

A crowd assembles near the bandstand.
RICK SHALE COLLECTION

1899 - 1909

The midway featured the Figure-Eight coaster. Burt's Ice Cream stand was nearby.
CHARLES J. JACQUES, JR. COLLECTION

assembled for a meeting and declared a dividend of 2.5 percent. Prior to this all profits had been used to make improvements on the line and in the park. After conducting the necessary business, the directors adjourned to Idora to have dinner and watch the diving horses Powder Face and Cupid.

Animals were a popular attraction at Idora for many years. At the end of July a diving elk joined the diving horses. The park also maintained a deer paddock, a small zoo with badgers and wildcats, and a bear pit with two trained bears named Dewey and Susan.

Company and group picnics were from the start a key element in increasing profits, and the streetcar company advertised the advantages of holding organized outings in the park. Since Idora Park was adjacent to Mill Creek Park, patrons were encouraged to sample both the novelties of the former and the natural beauty of the latter in a single excursion. These company picnics often included a program of races and athletic contests with many local merchants supplying prizes. At one picnic in 1901 participants in the bicycle race received a first prize of adjustable handle bars and a second prize of $2.00 of bicycle repairs from the Warner Brothers, who ran a bicycle repair shop in Youngstown. A few years later these same Warner Brothers left the bicycle business to begin a career in motion pictures.

Jack Warner reminisced about his family's Youngstown days in his autobiography *My First Hundred Years In Hollywood*, published in 1965. His older brother Sam had learned how to operate a movie projector and had found work in an amusement park in Chicago projecting Hale's Tours (early motion picture travelogues where patrons sat in a simulated train car.) Warner wrote, "When we sent word that there would soon be a kinetoscope Hale's Tours show at the Idora Amusement Park in Youngstown, Sam rushed home from Chicago. He got the projectionist job at Idora, and it didn't take long to sell the entire family on this magic medium which was drawing hundreds of patrons to the park every night."

The Park & Falls motormen had discovered that the Market Street viaduct was a good place to make up for lost time when returning to Central Square, and Superintendent Ivory soon found himself fielding complaints about the streetcars

An $8,000 electric merry-go-round was installed in 1899.
MAHONING VALLEY HISTORICAL SOCIETY

16

speeding on the bridge. In 1901 he issued orders that the cars were not to cross the bridge in less than one minute. The cars would slow up at the south end of the viaduct, and the motorman would wait for a two-bell signal from the conductor before proceeding over the bridge into the center of town.

Visitors to Idora on Labor Day weekend in 1901 could amuse themselves with dancing in the afternoon and evening to music provided by the Mahoning Orchestra, vaudeville performances in the Casino Theater, band concerts each afternoon, and the spectacle of the daredevil Gifford, who rode a bicycle off a ninety-foot tower into five feet of water. The newspaper reported that many patrons "were seen with kodaks and paper taking views and painting pictures of pretty places now so grand."

In October 1901 came the announcement that the Ingersoll Engineering & Construction Company of Pittsburgh would begin construction of a roller coaster at Idora fulfilling the promise management had made in 1899. It was not surprising that the contract went to Frederick Ingersoll. Like most of the Park & Falls directors, he was from western Pennsylvania, and he was one of the most respected coaster builders in the country. For the past several years Ingersoll, president of the Ingersoll Company, had been building small figure-eight coasters all over the country. He followed his installation at Idora with coasters at Kennywood Park in Pittsburgh and Conneaut Lake Park in Conneaut Lake, Pennsylvania. He also built entire parks such as Cleveland's Luna Park in 1904 and Pittsburgh's Luna Park in 1905.

Frederick Ingersoll was one of the most important innovators and builders

Frederick Ingersoll of Pittsburgh built Idora's first roller coaster, a Figure-Eight, in 1902.
MAHONING VALLEY HISTORICAL SOCIETY

1899 - 1909

The original dance pavilion.
MAHONING VALLEY HISTORICAL SOCIETY

Lucy Huffman wrote "The Idora March" in 1902.
MAHONING VALLEY HISTORICAL SOCIETY

in these formative years of amusement parks. John Miller, the most famous coaster designer from 1900 through the 1920s, said in 1929: "To my idea, Ingersoll was the tree from which the amusement limbs branched forth. All the leading park men came from that tree one way or another. The outdoor amusement field owes its very existence to him."

Ingersoll called his wooden coasters Three-way Figure-Eight Toboggan-Slides. For approximately $10,000, he would supply the toboggan complete in every detail, including ten cars, electrical wiring, a Westinghouse motor, and an office room. Ingersoll's advertising claimed "Our Figure-Eight Roller Coasters a World Beater." The new Idora Park coaster occupied a plot of ground 85 feet wide by 225 feet long and was built south of the carousel on the southwest side of the park near the slope toward Mill Creek Park. The cars ran on a hard maple track, and the structure was made of long-leaf Georgia pine.

"Don't fail to try the Toboggan Slide" read the ads. The new coaster was the highlight of the 1902 season; however, its location across the midway from the open-air theater required a new policy. The Casino Theater had been built considerably south of Parkview Avenue, no doubt to shield it from the noise of the arriving and departing trolley cars. When the new coaster proved disruptive to the theater patrons seated on the nearby hill, Manager Stanley declared that it would not operate while a performance was in progress.

Ingersoll also supplied Idora with a Laughing Gallery, which contained glass mirrors that provided humorously distorted reflections. Other attractions that summer included acrobat skits and a comedian in blackface. Daredevil acts were always popular; Lionel Legare and his mammoth Spiral Tower was advertised as "the boldest of all death-defying desperate acts." The Great Barlow Minstrels entertained in the Casino Theater for 5- and 10-cent admissions. Later in the season a local man Charles Leedy made a good impression with his vaudeville act of singing, dancing, whistling, and baton and gun juggling. Leedy would later become a prominent columnist, first for the *Youngstown Telegram* and then for the *Vindicator*.

Music in many forms continued to play an important role at Idora. Band concerts, especially by military bands, were always popular, and the dancing pavilion under the management of Col. Frank Sourbeck offered afternoon and evening dancing. The vaudeville acts in the Casino Theater always included some musical numbers. The park even inspired some music. In 1902 Lucy Huffman, wife of a local oculist, wrote "The Idora March," a two-step.

Idora did its best business on the holidays; on Decoration Day, the Fourth of July, and Labor Day the Park & Falls Company ran cars every three minutes to handle the immense crowds. A dining hall and food stands were set up to serve the hungry visitors. In charge of refreshments was Harry Burt, later famous as the inventor of the Good Humor ice cream bar. Burt's Ice Cream was a favorite with Youngstowners, who could purchase the treat at Burt's downtown facility on Phelps Street or at Idora.

Even with the new coaster and a well-patronized dancing pavilion and theater, Idora faced competition. One threat came from train excursions to nearby amusement parks. In 1902 the Lake Shore Railroad advertised trips to Woodland Beach Park on Lake Erie in Ashtabula Harbor, Ohio; Lakeside Park in Stoneboro, Pennsylvania; Exposition Park (later Conneaut Lake Park) in Conneaut Lake, Ohio; Waldameer Park in Erie, Pennsylvania; Euclid Beach Park in Cleveland; and Monarch Park in Oil City, Pennsylvania.

Many of the park's visitors were so attracted to Youngstown's south side that they chose to live in the area rather than just visit. Located away from the smoke and dirt of the steel mills, Idora became the breathing place for Youngstown, and a building boom began. "Blackberry 'patches' were converted into velvety lawns," observed the *Telegram* in 1901, "and aged orchards gave way to flower beds and garden plots. Like trees growing along a river in a desert, new houses sprang up along the route of the Park & Falls line from the Market Street viaduct to Mill Creek Park. Then the building boom spread laterally and new cross streets were opened and real estate dealers made the South Side the Mecca of home seekers." The Youngstown Consolidated Gas & Electric Company, which sold power to the streetcar line, also sold electricity to these new homeowners. And more residents meant more riders for the trolley line. In this way Idora contributed to the economic development of Youngstown.

One notable visitor to Idora in 1903 was Carrie Nation, the hatchet-wielding temperance fighter and saloon smasher. On July 7th the fifty-seven-year-old crusader addressed the Idora audience describing her career in the "smashing business" and urging them to regard the evils of drinking and smoking. "I have quit smashing saloons and have gone after the cause," she told the crowd. "It is political."

Samuel Grier, the Park & Falls president who had opposed a merger in 1900, died on January 3, 1904. He and his partners had built the streetcar line into a very profitable franchise, and larger companies again began to see the Park & Falls line as a potential acquisition.

Decoration Day 1904 drew twenty-five thousand people despite some rain. Professor B. Beck's Orchestra entertained the dancers, and the vaudeville bill starred the Flood Brothers, who, despite the name, were a father-and-son acrobatic team. Ed Stanley returned for his sixth and final season as park manager, and Harry Burt again took charge of the dining services. In 1904 the Ingersoll Company supplied Idora with a Fantasmagraph, described as a German invention that was the cleverest and most up-to-date amusement device.

The 1905 season brought several changes in management. Frank Melville, a New York impresario, leased Idora's Casino Theater and assigned H. D. Noble to be his local manager. Melville leased a dozen theaters and booked acts into about fifty parks. Frank Sourbeck continued to manage the dancing pavilion. Col. J. H. Dietrick, a former newspaperman who looked after attractions of the Ingersoll Pleasure Amusement Company of Pittsburgh, became manager of Idora, replacing Ed Stanley, who became manager of rival Avon Park. Pat Duffy, Sr. also began to work at Idora in 1905, an association that would continue for the next sixty-one years.

Each season seemed to bring a new novelty, and among the fresh attractions

Ed Stanley was manager for Idora Park's first six seasons.
MAHONING VALLEY HISTORICAL SOCIETY

Circle Swing and Figure-Eight.
B. DEREK SHAW COLLECTION

1899 - 1909

Some park employees lived in tent cottages during the summer.
DICK McKEE COLLECTION

This Idora photo gallery portrait included Winter Trigg (top), the park policeman.
DICK McKEE COLLECTION

supplied by the Ingersoll Company was the "Mysterious House," which had gained popularity the previous season in Cleveland and Pittsburgh.

School children on an outing to Idora in 1905 listed as their favorites the roller coaster, the carousel, and the Mysterious House. Trolleys were by far the most important form of transportation in 1905, but automobiles began to appear on streets around the park. A June 1905 headline read "Automobile Fever Spreading," and the accompanying story revealed that Youngstown had sixty-five autos.

Ownership of the park shifted in 1906 when the Park & Falls line was taken over by the Mahoning & Shenango Railway and Light Company. This company was the result of a merger on February 24, 1906, of the Pennsylvania & Mahoning Valley Railway and the Youngstown-Sharon Railway & Light Company. The board of directors was dominated by men from New York City, and a New Yorker E. N. Sanderson was elected president. The vice-president, however, was a local man, Randall Montgomery, a former mayor and city councilman in Youngstown as well as a former state legislator. In February 1899 he had resigned as president of the Board of City Commissioners to become general manager of the lighting companies in Youngstown. Within two years Montgomery had become president of the Youngstown Gas & Electric Company, which supplied power to the several streetcar lines operating in the Youngstown area.

Montgomery was also a partner with Willis H. Park and Harry G. Hamilton in the South Side Land and Improvement Company that developed the properties along the Park & Falls line. After Park and Hamilton built the Youngstown-Sharon line in 1901, Montgomery became general manager of seven companies in the Youngstown-Sharon area. Five years later when the Mahoning & Shenango Railway and Light Company assumed control of all traction companies in the area, Montgomery became its vice-president.

By April 1906 the Park & Falls line, which retained its identity despite the merger, installed a new board of directors and elected new officers. The new president was M. E. McCaskey, and the new vice-president was Randall Montgomery.

The change in ownership did not seem to affect operations at Idora Park, although Ed Kane replaced J. H. Dietrick as Idora's manager. The merger was part of nationwide consolidation in the street railway industry. New lines were being constructed and old lines extended. Americans were finding it easier to travel greater distances, and this meant parks could no longer take local residents for granted. The Erie Railroad stirred the wrath of local park men by offering 25-cent round trip fares to Cleveland. All the railroads offered excursions to such places as Niagara Falls and Atlantic City.

By 1906 the dance crowds had far outgrown the capacity of Idora's first dancing pavilion, and the park announced plans to construct a new, larger pavilion. The old dance hall was to be remodeled into a dining area, and the old dining hall torn down. The *Vindicator* noted that the dancing pavilion had never been adequate for the crowds it attracted. Dancing was a lucrative part of park business, and with a new building the company hoped to double its dance revenue. Plans called for the new pavilion to be ready by the following summer, but due perhaps to the depression and economic slowdown following the Panic of 1907, the dance hall would not be erected until 1910.

In August 1906 the Casino Theater booked John L. Sullivan for a week. The great bareknuckle boxing champion from 1882 to 1892 had been on the vaudeville circuit since retiring from the ring and was a frequent visitor to Youngstown. He traveled with a sparring partner and put on exhibition bouts in addition to his monologue. He also brought a picture machine to Idora with views of the McCoy-Corbett fight. Referring to the old champion's fondness for alcohol, the *Vindicator* wrote, "After retiring from the ring Sullivan fought the booze game for several years but of late has braced up and is doing something useful, using himself as a horrible example of what a man does when he is down and out." Sullivan's matinee performances cost 10 and 20 cents with evening performances set at 10, 20, and 30 cents.

By 1907 the Mahoning & Shenango Railway and Light Company, now the owner of Idora Park, controlled 150 miles of track in the two valleys. Sixteen separate companies were controlled by the parent corporation, and their twelve hundred employees drew a total annual salary of about $750,000. Ed Kane resigned as manager and was replaced by Bob Cunningham, who ordered several improvements for the 1907 season. George G. Rose, listed as excursion agent and superintendent of Idora Park, became the park manager in 1908 and served in that capacity for two seasons.

The open-air Casino Theater was roofed, and canvas walls were installed to protect patrons from rain and wind. Opera chairs were installed in the reserved-seat section to give the patrons a level of comfort similar that experienced at the Hippodrome and other downtown Youngstown theaters. Keith and Proctor's booking agency in New York supplied the vaudeville acts.

The park's drinking fountains were equipped with cooling devices to provide cold water, and more flowers were planted. Idora also offered an automobile sightseeing tour. Cars were becoming more popular, but most people could not yet afford to buy one. Nearly all visitors to the park still came by streetcar, but the park's auto tour was one way everyone could experience this newer method of transportation.

Celebrities were always popular, and in June 1908 the erstwhile baseball player turned evangelist Billy Sunday came to Idora to preach. "I don't care whether you like my sermon or not—I'm not here candidating," he told the crowd of four thousand that jammed into the Casino Theater. "Everybody who is decent will like it." He exhorted the audience to turn away from drinking, card-playing, and theater-going and objected to Sunday baseball, complacent Christians, and even Carnegie libraries, which he felt lacked "the old time religious spirit." Large dishpans were passed through the crowd to receive the collection. Most of the ministers in the area attended, and the paper reported that two-thirds of the audience were women.

Idora Park's tenth anniversary was marked by little fanfare, but the owners must have been gratified by the positive public response. Idora was clearly the area's primary location for summertime entertainment. Visitors could experience rides such as the toboggan coaster, merry-go-round, and circle swing; play games of pool, billiards, or box ball; and enjoy dancing, vaudeville, and free concerts.

Park & Falls summer cars at the Idora trolley station.
RICK SHALE COLLECTION

1910 - 1920

3 A NEW ERA

According to the ads and newspaper articles, the 1910 season was the beginning of "a new era" for Idora Park. They referred to the park as the New Idora. Most prominent among the changes was a gigantic new dance pavilion, whose construction had been announced four years earlier. This huge structure was designed by Angus S. Wade, a noted Philadelphia architect. The dance hall, or ballroom, was open air, and a porch ran around all four sides of the building. Large awnings could be raised or lowered to take advantage of a summer breeze or to protect the patrons from inclement weather. The roof was accented by a series of cupolas, and the main entrance on the western side, which faced a new streetcar stop, had a Moorish style.

The dance pavilion opened for the first time on June 20, 1910, and attracted a huge crowd. The *Youngstown Telegram* reported that the dance floor was the largest in Ohio, measuring 238 by 96 feet. It was noted with some pride that this was even larger than the pavilion at Coney Island in New York. The floor and acoustic quality were far superior to the old dance pavilion, and the design included large checkrooms and toilet facilities near the entrance. A refreshment stand was built opposite the entrance, and tables were arranged so that patrons could sit and watch the dancers. Nellie James, daughter of park policeman Winter Trigg, was hired as cashier, a position that she would hold for forty-six years.

Thousands attended the first night. The *Telegram* reported that "a grand march was the opening feature of the new pavilion and hundreds of young people took part. It ended in an old fashioned quadrille and circle two step." Palms decorated the building for the opening, and the newspaper reported that eight hundred couples occupied the dance floor with room for twice that number without crowding. Professor Boyle's Orchestra played. The exterior of the building was equally spectacular, and the *Telegram* declared, "When lighted with electric bulbs on all the cornices and towers at night, it is both picturesque and brilliant."

To serve the patrons of the new dance hall, the streetcar company extended the trolley tracks down the western side of the park and created a turn-around loop and shelter where passengers could disembark and walk directly up a short hill to the dance pavilion entrance, which faced Mill Creek Park. This trolley loop was beautifully landscaped and contained a small lagoon with ducks and goldfish. To avoid congestion, the company built a second station for streetcars a few hundred yards north where the passengers

The Youngstown Vindicator, May 28, 1910, announced the opening of the park's new ballroom.
MAHONING VALLEY HISTORICAL SOCIETY

boarded the trolley cars to return home. A path between the Figure-Eight coaster and the carousel ran from the midway to this loading station.

Passengers rode to and from Idora in open-air "summer cars." As the *Vindicator* explained, "these were 'open face' cars with no sides. The seats were reversible benches; one chose his bench and reached it by mounting a running board, which ran along the whole length of the car. Sometimes, when the dance 'let out,' lingerers had to ride precariously on the running board, the conductor climbing around them to collect fares. . . ."

Other attractions in 1910 included the roller skating rink and circle swing. Invented by Harry Traver, the circle swing featured several cars or wicker gondolas suspended by cables from arms that revolved around a tall central mast. The *Vindicator* noted that despite the movement and glare of electric lights, robins had nested at the top of the circle swing. Charles D. Hoover ran the photo gallery. He was an artist as well as a photographer and maintained studios on Market Street in Youngstown and at Idora Park. The ever-popular vaudeville acts were booked through the American Vaudeville Agency of New York, but some summer stock was also provided. The Horne Stock Company, led by Col. Frank Horne, performed *Double Trouble* in June.

Although most visitors still came to the park by trolley, in 1910 Idora for the first time set aside a section of the park for auto parking. The newspapers reported that this lot was "crowded each evening with machines." Youngstown now had more than 600 automobiles, a ten-fold increase from five years earlier.

The new open-air ballroom featured ornate architecture.
RICK SHALE COLLECTION

The landscaped lagoon and station were just a few steps from the ballroom.
RICK SHALE COLLECTION

23

1910 - 1920

The lagoon was transformed into a lily pond.
RICHARD L. BOWKER COLLECTION

Idora held Harvest Moon dances in the fall.
EDWARD C. LEARNER COLLECTION

Presiding over the New Idora Park was Perry Barge, who replaced George Rose as Idora's manager. Barge had formerly been in charge of Cascade Park in New Castle, Pennsylvania, which was also operated by the Mahoning & Shenango Railway and Light Company. As the park continued to grow, maintaining order became more important. The management made every effort to keep the park free of troublemakers, and signs were placed around the park reading: "This is a private park. The management reserves the right to exclude any person from the grounds." No fence encircled Idora, and the task of keeping the undesirable element out of the open grounds fell to the park's own police force.

Special arrangements were made to accommodate the large Fourth of July crowds. An extra theater performance was scheduled, and dancing and roller skating began at 10 a.m. The vaudeville bill consisted of Will Lacy doing his comedy bicycle act; Amy Shaffer and Company performing *The Girl Spy of Dixie*; Pongo & Leo, a comedy Pole act; Olivia & Fanny Marchio, Italian street singers; and the Petching Brothers, a musical act. One notable change was the absence of fireworks. A rash of injuries had prompted many city residents to campaign for laws restricting or licensing fireworks. Manager Barge called for a sane Fourth and banned fireworks from the park. The newspaper noted that "Those who desire amusement and a quiet time amid the cool breezes at the park will find Idora the place."

Youngstown's population had grown from about 45,000 in 1900 to nearly 80,000 in 1910, and so many of these residents settled on Youngstown's south side that a new high school was needed. In 1911 South High School (Youngstown's second) opened on Market Street at Warren Avenue where the streetcar made its turn toward Idora.

The Park & Falls line and its parent company the Mahoning & Shenango Railway and Light Company, continued to lease the Idora property, though actual title to the land changed. In 1910 and 1911 Willis H. Park, one of the streetcar company's directors at the time Idora was conceived, purchased title to the property from Col. L. T. Foster and his wife Susanna. Willis H. Park and later his estate would hold title until 1923.

The 1911 season brought yet another change in management. Royal Platt replaced Barge and became the fifth manager in seven years. Platt, however, would remain in that post for a decade and would oversee great changes in Idora.

The new dance pavilion enabled the park to host additional musical events, and in June 1911 the Youngstown Music Festival Association engaged the pavilion for a two-day event. The Theodore Thomas Orchestra was booked, and the Youngstown Festival Choir sang *The Messiah*.

Bowling was popular with the Idora crowd, and Hooks Morgan was again in charge of the Idora bowling alley. Vaudeville reigned at the Casino Theater, but the structure was not yet enclosed, so rain would wash out performances. The park replaced its original Dentzel carousel with a newer model from the same company. This new merry-go-round featured animals that moved up and down as the machine revolved.

Consolidation continued in the transportation and power industries as smaller companies were absorbed by larger corporations. On June 28, 1911, the Republic Railway and Light Company was incorporated in Trenton, New Jersey, with a capital of $17.5 million dollars. The new company gained control of twenty-eight electric light, gas, power, and street railway companies in the Mahoning and

Shenango Valleys. The Associated Press reported that one of the specific aims of the new company had been to acquire the outstanding stock of the Mahoning & Shenango Railway and Light Company. This change in ownership did not affect Idora Park. Republic Railway and Light, as a holding company, became the controlling financial organization, and Mahoning & Shenango Railway and Light continued as the operating division.

Billboard, the entertainment trade paper, summarized Idora in 1912: attractions included a coaster, circle swing, carousel, photo gallery, arcade, theater, dance pavilion, roller skating, bowling alley and billiard parlor. These rides were fairly standard in trolley parks around the country. Most park owners or operators attended annual trolley park shows where they got ideas for new attractions. Major ride builders and manufacturers such as T. M. Harton, William Dentzel Company, the Philadelphia Toboggan Company, Cagney Brothers, Allan Herschell Company, and J. W. Zarro Company would display their latest creations at these shows.

The Keith and Proctor Circuit supplied Idora with five vaudeville acts each week. For example, a July 1912 bill included a harmonic expert and paper manipulator, a singing and yodeling duo, gymnasts, a comedy quartet, and a monkey act. Idora drew an average of 5,000 visitors a day and big days such as Decoration Day, Fourth of July, Welsh Day, and Labor Day drew 18,000 to 25,000.

Idora's Casino Theater was renovated under the supervision of John Elliott, who had spent the previous five years managing the Park Theater owned by Willis H. Park. The stage was enlarged and new scenery installed. Matinee performances at the Casino Theater cost 10 cents; Sunday matinees had a range of 10 and 20 cents, and evening shows were 10, 20, and 30 cents.

Opening the 1913 season was comedian Herman Timberg, who headlined the five Keith vaudeville acts, but motion pictures also attracted attention. In addition to the live acts, the Casino Theater presented the Idoragraph, which projected the latest moving pictures. By 1913 there were several movie theaters in Youngstown (seven on Federal Street alone), and the Idoragraph was no doubt an attempt to draw some of these movie fans away from the downtown and out to the park.

In addition to its use by daily visitors, the dance pavilion became a popular location for private parties. The society news regularly carried announcements of these events such as the Masonic May Dance and the Knights of Columbus May parties. For the regular season Professor Boyle's twelve-piece orchestra returned for the sixth consecutive year to provide music. The tradition of holding a music festival in Idora's dance pavilion continued. The Chicago Symphony with conductor Frederick Stock opened the third annual festival June 3, 1913, with a work by Anton Dvořák and performed a Wagner concert the following night. The Youngstown Festival Choir directed by Prower Symons offered vocal selections. As in the previous years, the dance pavilion was temporarily converted to a concert hall by the addition of a stage for the orchestra and tiers of seats for the choir.

Animals continued to be popular with Idora's patrons. A decade earlier bears, deer, and other animals

Royal E. Platt and his collie Major. Platt managed Idora from 1911 to 1920.
DICK PLATT COLLECTION

Clowning in Idora's photo gallery.
MAHONING VALLEY HISTORICAL SOCIETY

1910 - 1920

A matinee crowd in front of Idora's Casino Theater.
RICK SHALE COLLECTION

The original Figure-Eight coaster was modified into a deep-dip railway designed and built by the McKay Construction Company.
COURTESY OF HISTORIC IMAGES AND DAVID W. FRANCIS COLLECTION

had been displayed, and the diving horses had drawn crowds. In 1914 the big attraction was the pony ride with Shetlands supplied by the Brookdale Pony Farm of Youngstown. A dozen ponies were used with half of them saddled and half drawing small rigs. The attraction proved immediately popular and three more ponies were added. Manager Platt announced that a brightly colored fence would be built around the one-eighth mile pony track.

New rides were an important means of attracting new business as well as retaining old customers, and so on December 2, 1913, the Park & Falls Street Railway Company signed a contract with the T. M. Harton Company of Pittsburgh, Pennsylvania, to build a new roller coaster. Additional land adjacent to the park was obtained from William Bakody, whose wife was Col. L. T. Foster's daughter and German Lanterman's granddaughter. Construction was begun, and the Dip-the-Dips was ready by opening day of the 1914 season. It was built on the eastern border of the park on the other side of the hill from the theater.

Theodore M. Harton, who lived in Pittsburgh, was a major force in the amusement park industry in the late 1890s and early 1900s. He built over fifty roller coasters in parks in the United States, England, and Europe including coasters in Conneaut Lake Park, Conneaut Lake, Pennsylvania; Coney Island, Cincinnati, Ohio; Celeron Park, Jamestown, New York; and Cedar Point, Sandusky, Ohio. Harton also owned parks such as West View in the North Hills section of Pittsburgh and Walbridge Park in Toledo, Ohio.

Harton's contract required Idora to provide part of the land to be used for the construction, an entrance to the new coaster, and six thousand kilowatts of electricity per month. In return, the park would receive for the first two years of the contract 20 percent of Harton's gross receipts. For the next three years the amount would increase to 22.5 percent of the gross, and for the remaining five years the figure would be increased again to 25 percent of the gross ticket sales.

The Dip-the-Dips coaster (or toboggan railway, as Harton called it) had a four thousand-foot long track constructed of yellow pine. No nails were used in the construction; instead, 250,000 bolts were used as fasteners. The trains moved at an average speed of twenty-three miles per hour, and the track was equipped with magnetic brakes and safety devices. A crowd of 10,000 attended the park on opening day, and the newspaper reported that 8,000 to 9,000 tried the new Dip-the-Dips.

By 1914 many trolley companies were no longer interested in owning and operating rides but were often willing to let "concessionaires" build and operate the

major rides under long-term (ten to fifteen-year) leases. To encourage construction of large rides like roller coasters, trolley parks often granted the coaster builders additional concessions to operate other rides in the parks. At Idora, for example, the T. M. Harton Company not only built and owned the Dips but also built the carousel building and owned and operated the carousel.

In 1914 Idora Park changed its entertainment policy and switched from vaudeville to legitimate theater. The Morton Opera Company was engaged for the summer to provide plays and proved quite popular with the Casino Theater crowd. Among their productions were *The Telephone Girl* and Gilbert and Sullivan's *H. M. S. Pinafore*. Prices climbed slightly with evening performances now scaled at 10, 20, 30, and 50 cents.

Many nations and ethnic groups were represented in Youngstown's growing population, and the nationality days that would become so popular in the coming decades were introduced at Idora Park. Welsh Day was already a tradition that annually drew crowds of 15,000 to 20,000. In 1914 when the Germans held their day at Idora, the main topic of discussion was the war in Europe.

The 1914 season was the most successful in Idora's history, and the traction company decided to make some major changes for 1915. More land was acquired that doubled the size of the park, and a new entrance was constructed. The success of the Morton Opera Company prompted many changes in the theater. The proscenium was enlarged by six feet, and several dressing rooms were built to accommodate the forty-member company, which was engaged for a second season of musical comedy. The front of the theater was redesigned, and above the stage a large gridiron or fly loft was built to handle larger pieces of scenery. This was probably also when the canvas sides of the theater were replaced with permanent wooden walls. Director Lewis Morton announced that his company would open with *Mary's Lamb* and follow with *Naughty Marietta, The Chocolate Soldier, Three Twins, Rose Maid, Mademoiselle Modiste, Red Rose, Spring Maid,* and *Firefly*. Raymond Crane returned as the company's leading man, and Maude Gray made her debut as leading lady.

The most visible change at Idora in 1915 was the addition of a new major ride, the Panama Canal. The real canal had opened August 15, 1914, and by the 1915 season the Philadelphia Toboggan Company (PTC), located in the Germantown section of Philadelphia, constructed a combination old mill and chute ride for Idora. For the next fifteen years PTC would be involved in the construction of all of Idora's other "major" rides. The Panama Canal was a water ride, constructed at a time when only a few of the leading parks in America had such an attraction. This ride clearly distinguished Idora from most of its small neighboring parks.

The *Vindicator* offered a detailed description of the new ride: "Standing right in the center of the park activities the mountains that have been built around and over the Panama Canal add greatly to the scenic effect. This is heightened by the great wheel which, driven by electricity, keeps the water flowing through the canal in a steady current. The current sends the gondolas around a winding course of 1,000 feet and then the 'lock' is reached. Here the boats are drawn up an incline plane and shoot suddenly down into a broader expanse of canal that might be termed 'Gatun Lake.' This is the culmination of the ride which

T. M. Harton, builder of the Dips coaster and carousel building.
CHARLES J. JACQUES, JR. COLLECTION

The heart of the park featured the carousel, photo studio, and rebuilt coaster.
RICK SHALE COLLECTION

1910 - 1920

The ballroom, July 4, 1916.
MARCELLA DUFFY COLLECTION

Interior of the ballroom.
CHARLES J. JACQUES, JR. COLLECTION

Visitors dressed up for a day at Idora.
MARCELLA DUFFY COLLECTION

weaves in and out a number of tunnels providing ample amusement and diversion." The Panama Canal was an early version of the Rapids, which the Philadelphia Toboggan Company would build on approximately the same location fifteen years later.

Idora's Panama Canal was put into the park as a leased concession and was owned by a group of investors. Among the owners were Henry B. Auchy, who was president of the Philadelphia Toboggan Company, and E. J. Lauterbach, who owned attractions in Dayton, Ohio; Pittsburgh, Pennsylvania; and Rye Beach, New York. Auchy, Lauterbach, and their partners conducted business under the name Idora Panama Canal Company, which was registered in Ohio, and operated the Canal as a concession in the park.

Construction of the "red mill," PTC's generic name for the Panama Canal, was supervised by a Mr. Pike, who traveled from Philadelphia to Youngstown. Over 16,500 feet of tongue and groove cypress wood were used for the channel, while the rest of the structure—the stringers, intermediates, bents on incline, ledgers, braces, runway, motor house, and pavilion—were made of long-leaf yellow pine. In addition, cedar posts were used to give the ride a rustic appearance. The plans and specifications, eight boats, and machinery for the red mill cost the partners $2,600. Construction added an additional $5,482.04 bringing the total to $8,082.04.

Other improvements in 1915 included renovation of the bowling alley and the conversion of the old roller skating rink into a first class dining room that could accommodate three hundred diners. The buildings were painted in the park colors of green and white. The new dining room was surrounded by wide verandahs, and the bandstand was moved closer so diners could enjoy a concert while they ate. Each Sunday, when dancing was prohibited, Professor Boyle's Orchestra gave hour-long concerts at 2 p.m., 4 p.m., 7 p.m., and 9 p.m. During these times the piano in the Penny Arcade was silent. On nights other than Sundays the band provided dance music in the pavilion.

Two changes were made for the dance pavilion: the starting and closing times in the evening were moved up thirty

minutes and dances would now run from 8:30 p.m. to 11:30 p.m. Since the theater performances generally got out at 11 p.m., the change in dancing time would alleviate the rush to get streetcars at the same time or would enable theater patrons to enjoy half an hour of dancing.

The other policy change was to ban all fancy dancing. In previous seasons Manager Platt had permitted some fancy dancing such as "The Boston" if it did not interfere with other patrons. But complaints prompted him to institute the ban in 1915. "This year none of the new creations will be permitted," explained the *Vindicator* and added "Similar action has been taken by the best of parks in all parts of the country." A month into the season, however, Platt yielded to the pleas of the young dancers and announced that the modern dances would be permitted one night a week. "That is, all new dances excepting trots," he explained. "As to trotting, that will not be permitted at all."

Rehearsing on the Casino Theater stage.
MARCELLA DUFFY COLLECTION

Strolling on the midway circa 1916.
MARCELLA DUFFY COLLECTION

1910 - 1920

Park employees.
EDWARD C. LEARNER COLLECTION

Aerial view of the carousel and Figure-Eight.
© THE VINDICATOR, 1999

On Monday nights those who favored the new steps could dance the tango, one step, and hesitation waltz; on the other five nights only the two-step, waltz, Cuban waltz, and schottische were allowed.

Idora began to solicit picnic business more aggressively. Four large, open picnic shelters were available, as was free use of gas grills so picnickers could warm food and make coffee. A baseball field was constructed for picnic groups, and the park announced that the field would be used by semi-pro teams on Sundays and holidays. Refreshment stands in the park supplied peanuts, popcorn, candy, and beverages.

In all, it was reported that the streetcar company and its concessionaires spent $30,000 to improve the park for the 1915 season. This was probably overstated since the report indicated that the Panama Canal cost $18,000 while the actual cost according to the files of the Philadelphia Toboggan Company was a little over $8,000. Admittedly the $8,000 did not include the usual markup for profit since it was partially owned by Auchy, who owned PTC, though it was a tradition in amusement parks to publicly inflate the cost of rides.

All these improvements anticipated a successful season, but when the park officially opened on Sunday, May 23, 1915, misfortune struck. The front-page headlines of the *Youngstown Telegram* Monday night read: "Pleasure Cars Meet at Frightful Speed In Mid Air Sunday." An opening-day accident on the Dip-the-Dips had claimed the life of one passenger and had injured nearly a score. The *Vindicator* offered the following account: "shouts of mirth were suddenly changed to shrieks of terror at Idora Park Sunday afternoon when passengers in a rapidly speeding car on the scenic railway dashed toward a three-car train ahead of them which had failed to mount the second ascent, and was backing up toward them. In a moment the two cars with their burden of human freight came together with a crash. One man was killed and sixteen others were more or less seriously hurt. The accident happened at 3:45 p.m. in full view of hundreds of spectators."

Dead was twenty-year-old Daniel Denehy of West Myrtle Avenue in Young-

The Panama Canal mill chute ride opened in 1915.
CHARLES J. JACQUES, JR. COLLECTION

stown, a clerk at the Western Union Telegraph office. The cause of death was listed as fractured skull and internal injuries, but how the accident occurred remained in dispute. Some witnesses said the crash itself did not cause the fatal injury and that Denehy was conscious and attempting to free himself from the wreckage. As he was being freed from the car pinning him to the track, he slipped through the track and fell about eighteen feet to the ground fracturing his skull. Denehy was riding alone in the front car because his female companion had been too slow to board the train and had been left at the station. Immediately behind Denehy sat his friends James Trahey and Hazel Dunn. Not until their train had reached the top of the first hill did the party realize that a collision was imminent. "Once again the handrails were gripped," reported the *Telegram*, "but this time fear and not pleasure impelled the move. Like a bullet the car dropped to meet the oncoming car at the bottom. The sickening crash followed. The seat in which Denehy was seated, also the one occupied by Trahey and Miss Dunn were smashed into kindling wood." The manager of the ride, who had fifteen years' experience, had no idea why the first train had failed to negotiate the second hill, which measured about ninety feet. He speculated that something on the bottom of the car had caused a drag that reduced the momentum. The ride was

The Canal ride featured mountainous scenic effects.
CHARLES J. JACQUES, JR. COLLECTION

equipped with safety devices that should have warned the operator that a train was in trouble, but these warning mechanisms apparently did not function.

Following the fatal accident, the Dips was closed pending an investigation, and the streetcar company, moving swiftly to distance itself from responsibility, issued the following statement: "The ride on which the accident occurred is not owned, operated or under the control of the Park & Falls Street Railway Company, owners and managers of Idora Park. In fact, the 'Dip the Dips' is not within the park at all, its only connection with Idora being that the entrance to the ride is from the park. The ride is operated by the T. M. Harton Company, of Pittsburgh, who own and operate rides

1910 - 1920

An opening-day accident claimed the life of one passenger on the Dips coaster in 1915.
MAHONING VALLEY HISTORICAL SOCIETY

The mill wheel and chainlift propelled boats through the Panama Canal.
CHARLES J. JACQUES, JR. COLLECTION

in nearly every large city in the country, and who leased the ground adjacent to Idora to build this ride...While having no connection or agreement with the Harton Company excepting to permit it to have an entrance to the ride from Idora, the park management, for its own information, is having a thorough investigation made into the accident.

Despite the street railway company's claim to the contrary, the T. M. Harton Company had a contract with Idora and was obviously a concessionaire in the park. Idora Park would never have permitted access to the coaster from the park if an agreement between the parties did not exist. If the coaster had merely been built on an adjoining piece of ground, Idora would have fenced it off. Idora's management did not acknowledge the existence of concessionaires (i.e. tenants), except under rare circumstances such as a major accident. Then the park owners tended to throw as much blame as possible on the concessionaire.

The mishap did not affect business on the park's other coaster, which continued to operate at full capacity with passengers seemingly oblivious to the tragedy that had occurred at the park's southeast corner. T. M. Harton himself, who was fifty-two years old at the time of the accident, traveled from Pittsburgh to Youngstown to inspect the Dips and, in hopes of quieting the newspapers and reassuring the public, ordered the installation of additional safety devices. As part of the new safety plan, a man was stationed in the cupola at the top of the chainlift where he could see the entire track; a switchboard enabled him to control any car on the lift hill. Youngstown City Council ordered Safety Director Harry Parrock and Building Inspector C. C. Knox to inspect the ride, and they pronounced it "as safe as human ingenuity can make it." The accident did not seem to hurt attendance; a crowd of fourteen thousand came to the park on Decoration Day, the day the Dips reopened, and patronized the attraction as if nothing had happened.

By 1915 more than 3,300 auto licenses had been issued in Youngstown, and more and more patrons came to Idora by car or gasoline-powered passenger buses called jitneys. To make up for the lost streetcar revenue, the management announced its intention to charge a ten-cent admission to the park for those not arriving by trolley. The jitney drivers, organized as the Youngstown Street Bus Association, bitterly opposed the pay-as-you-enter plan and threatened to invoke the largely ignored blue laws and shut down Sunday amusement business. In late July the jitney drivers made good on their threat, and seven employees of Idora including Manager Royal Platt and the operators of the Dips, Panama Canal, merry-go-round, Figure-Eight coaster, and bowling alley were arrested. One week later the charges were dismissed on a legal technicality.

In June 1915 Idora Park became the setting for a locally filmed motion picture titled *The Princess' Visit to Youngstown*. The Princess, played by Agnes Laing, was shown boarding a Park & Falls streetcar in downtown Youngstown, journeying to Idora, and touring the park with Manager Platt. Later scenes showed the Princess visiting Southern Park to watch auto races and an airplane exhibition.

A new roller skating rink located in the northeastern corner of the park was erected for the 1916 season. Idora had converted the old rink to a dining hall in 1915, which had temporarily eliminated the popular sport. The new rink had a 60-

by 130-foot maple floor, and music was provided by a $2,000 military band organ. The new rink was located near the picnic pavilions where patrons could again enjoy the use of free gas to cook their food. Picnickers were welcome to play on the baseball field, which was also used by the Em-an-Ess League, an organization of eight teams from different divisions of the Mahoning & Shenango Railway and Light Company.

Following the accident on the Dips, some of the injured parties filed suit, naming the Park & Falls Street Railway Company and the T. M. Harton Company as joint defendants. In 1916 the victims of the accident received judgments in Common Pleas Court against the operators of the Dips. To satisfy these judgments, the Sheriff sold the Dips for $10,000 to Attorney Harold Hull, representing the victims. The *Vindicator* reported that "it is understood that the judgment creditors will form a company and operate the 'Dip the Dips.' Such profits as are made will be used to pay the claims of the various judgment creditors which amount to over $7,000." A few days after the sale, however, the attorney refused to accept title, claiming a violation of the statute that required a ten-day notice of the sale to be posted. Attorney Hull further claimed that the Park & Falls Street Railway Company received profits from the Dips and was thus a joint tort feasor with the company owning the Dips. The sale was voided, and two weeks later Hull again bought the Dips but this time paid only $7,050. Attorney Hull strongly objected to Idora's actions of boarding up the entrance to the Dips and threatened court action to reopen the entrance. Idora in turn announced that the Philadelphia Toboggan Company, which had built the Panama Canal ride, would construct a Race Through the Clouds coaster for the park. The Dips, it was explained, had ceased to be in any way an attraction at Idora.

In the end, the Philadelphia Toboggan Company did not build a Race Through the Clouds coaster. An accommodation was reached with Attorney Hull, for the Park & Falls Street Railway Company became the owners of the Dips. The accident and court case appear to have terminated T. M. Harton's interest in the Dips coaster, but the Harton Company, doing business as the Toboggan Amusement Company, did retain an interest in part of the land on which the coaster was built as well as the concession for the carousel.

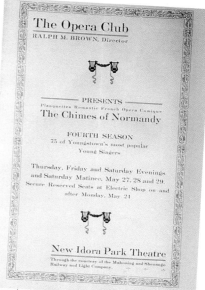

The Dip-the-Dips coaster built by T. M. Harton.
CHARLES J. JACQUES, JR. COLLECTION

1910 - 1920

The loading station of the Panama Canal, built by the Philadelphia Toboggan Company.
CHARLES J. JACQUES, JR. COLLECTION

T. M. Harton would die of influenza in 1919, four years after the accident. In the record of his estate was the Idora Park Caroussel [sic] and Building, which was appraised at $7,500, and the Toboggan Amusement Company, valued at $6,600. The carousel building that Harton's company had built remained in use until Idora closed.

The Morton Musical Comedy Company returned to the Casino Theater in 1916 for a third and final season and opened with *The Red Rose*, which the *Vindicator* pronounced "a corking show." "The company this summer," the paper explained, "is a musical comedy company, a company of singing and dancing players rather than operatic vocalists. There is a distinction. It seems that opera has served its day so far as the average audience is concerned and that musical comedy has taken its place and the newest form of entertainment is to be the policy at Idora. 'The Red Rose' is a romance set to music, with a lot of comedy of the hit-and-run sort and plenty of color. It is a fast snappy story and with any number of amusing character types for portrayal. It permits of some gorgeous costuming and this opportunity has certainly been grasped while scenically the production is all that anyone could ask." Margaret Devon was the prima donna, Henry Coote the tenor, and Walter Wills the comedian. Director Lewis Morton assured patrons that each production would include twenty beautiful chorus girls.

The Park & Falls line added another car in 1916. It had the standard green exterior with a light oak and buff interior. Mazda lamps lit the car, and the seats, arranged longitudinally, held fifty passengers. The company had long needed extra storage space for its cars and announced plans to erect new car barns on the property presently occupied by Wright Field, the city's premier athletic field on West Federal Street. To replace Wright Field, the small baseball diamond at Idora was transformed into an elaborate facility with a grandstand and bleachers. Eight city lots adjoining the park were purchased to allow this expansion. The transaction proved doubly advantageous: the street railway company got a centrally located property for its car barns, and it shifted the location of major sporting events from downtown Youngstown to Idora.

In 1917, the dance policy was liberalized. Fancy dancing, heretofore allowed only on Monday nights, would now be permitted Monday, Tuesday, and Thursday nights and Saturday afternoons. Boyle's Concert Band again provided dance music. A new, large parking lot for autos was constructed adjacent to the dance pavilion.

Summer stock again held sway at the theater, and the Horne Stock Company replaced the Morton Musical Comedy troupe. Col. Horne announced that Beulah Poynter would be his leading lady. Among the selections for 1917 were: *Brewster's Millions, Common Clay, Mile-a-Minute Kendall, It Pays To Advertise, Rolling Stones, Broadway and Buttermilk, Treasure Island,* and *The Fortune Hunter.*

World War I affected the community, and in late August a great send-off for Youngstown's Base Hospital Unit was held at Idora prior to their departure for Europe. Two parades, athletic contests, a program of patriotic speeches, and fireworks drew a crowd of twenty thousand to the park.

The war in Europe occupied the headlines in the spring of 1918, and Idora opened the season with a series of patriotic concerts. The Horne Stock Company and Boyle's Orchestra were engaged again in 1918. After several delays, the baseball field finally was enlarged, graded, and fenced, and grandstands were erected. The inaugural game at what was now the area's best athletic field was played on June 8th.

Patriotism was emphasized throughout the 1918 season. A crowd of 35,000 to 40,000 visited the park on July 4th, and the highlight of the season was a July 28th concert by John Philip Sousa and his band. Sousa, already regarded as the world's most famous bandmaster, had taken his group on a world tour to entertain troops but had been granted a leave of absence to perform a summer concert tour. Thousands attended Idora's Casino Theater to hear Sousa's performance. His marches such as the "Stars and Stripes Forever" and "El Capitan" drew the longest applause.

July 18, 1918, marked the passing of Willis H. Park, one of Idora's founders. Park had extensive real estate dealings, and was one of the town's most prominent businessmen. In 1910 and 1911 he had purchased the land on which Idora Park was located. In addition to Idora Park, he formed and operated several real estate companies and a lumber company and built Willis Park (an athletic field) and the Park Theater, both of which were named for him.

Idora continued to acquire new rides and attractions. A Mangels Whip was added in 1919. This ride was designed by William F. Mangels of Coney Island, New York. Until 1914 Mangels had built galloping-horse carousels and mechanical shooting galleries, but with his invention of the Whip he expanded his ride manufacturing business into iron rides. (Unlike gravity rides such as wooden roller coasters, iron rides were constructed of iron or steel and operated at ground level.) He advertised the Whip in *Billboard* as "the latest amusement ride, combines thrill, action, pleasure, and safety. Large returns on moderate investments."

The Whip, which became a staple in amusement parks across the country, was an electrically operated iron ride that consisted of twelve cars traveling along an oblong track. While the cars were on the straight or longer part of the course, they had a moderate speed, but as the cars reached the ends of the ride, the speed greatly increased and centrifugal force caused the cars to "Snap the Curve."

By 1919 visitors to Idora's improved baseball diamond had seen some memorable contests. In August the Pittsburgh Pirates came to Idora for an exhibition game. Opposing the big leaguers was a local semi-pro team, the McElroys, managed by Mickey Stambaugh and sponsored by the McElroy Furniture Store. The Pirates shut out the locals 6-0, but in the coming years the McElroys would provide stiff competition for several major league clubs.

The ballpark was used for other athletic contests, and boxing was a particular draw. In the final outdoor bout of the 1919 season the Chicago lightweight Charley White met Tony Zill of Niles and gave the local favorite a sound beating.

Over the years Idora was the site of many political rallies, and one of the most memorable occurred in 1919. In September the Irish leader Eamonn DeValera came to Youngstown to promote the cause of Irish freedom. After attending mass, DeValera and his associate Harry Boland were escorted to Idora Park by a large contingent of local officials and police. When they arrived at the Casino Theater, the crowd was so large that the rally had to be shifted to the outdoor amphitheater in Mill Creek Park.

The 1920s were the decade of the "aeroplane" as barnstormers and Lindbergh's Atlantic crossing captured the public's imagination. In 1920 Idora updated its circle swing by replacing the old wicker baskets with small airplanes.

Also in 1920 the old Three-Way Figure-Eight Toboggan coaster, which had been built by the Ingersoll Company in

John Philip Sousa visited Idora in 1918.
RICK SHALE COLLECTION

1910 - 1920

The Firefly roller coaster replaced the deep-dip railway in 1920.
© THE VINDICATOR, 1999

1902 and modified over the years, was replaced with the Firefly coaster. This new side-friction coaster was similar in design to the old Figure-Eight but was higher and had deeper dips. A common practice in amusement parks across the country was to replace older coasters with rebuilt, updated versions of the same attraction. Idora's "new" coaster was built on the same ground as the Figure-Eight and used the old coaster's loading station. It became an instant favorite with Idora's visitors.

The postwar years were good for Idora's business. In 1920 Manager Platt declared the opening day crowd of fifteen thousand the largest in the park's history. The amusement park continued to be a location where people of different classes and nationalities could mix. A reporter covering the opening day noted that "Youngstown's polyglot population is well represented: you hear scraps of Italian and wonder what other languages are represented in the unknown phrases which attract the ear." Most attractions at Idora presented no language barrier to the immigrants who were beginning to swell Youngstown's population.

In 1920 the Mahoning & Shenango Railway and Light Company changed its name to the Penn-Ohio Electric Company, though it was still controlled by the Republic Railway and Light Company. Later that year Penn-Ohio Electric transferred its power properties and some of its transit properties including the Park & Falls line to a subsidiary called the Penn-Ohio Power and Light Company. (Ten years later, on June 23, 1930, Penn-Ohio Power would transfer the Park & Falls line to the Youngstown Municipal Railway. On July 2, 1930, Penn-Ohio Power, along with other properties, would be sold and consolidated as Ohio Edison.)

The new season was marred by tragedy when eighteen-year-old John Hoover, who ran the shooting gallery, was shot and killed. No one witnessed the accident, but police speculated that a customer preparing to shoot a target at the gallery may have pulled the trigger prematurely, hit young Hoover, and fled in panic. After being shot, Hoover was first carried to the Photo Gallery run by his father, Charles D. Hoover, and then transported to the hospital by his brother Paul Hoover, who also worked in the park. He died shortly after arriving at the hospital.

Five weeks later another park employee was killed. F. M. Martin, the manager of the new Firefly coaster, was inspecting the track when he was struck by a car, knocked to a lower track, and then hit by another car.

The Horne Stock Company returned for another season, and the cast contained a new leading lady, Lillian Desmonde, who would become the most popular actress to appear on the stage at Idora Park. With uncanny prescience the *Vindicator* reported that "Miss Desmond [sic] seems destined to become a great favorite with Idora patrons." In fact, she would dominate the legitimate theater in the park for the next decade.

By 1920 Idora Park had the only fenced-in ball field in Youngstown, and the city's premier semi-pro team, the McElroys, again used Idora as their home field. In July the legendary John McGraw brought his New York Giants to Idora. Though the New York lineup included five future members of baseball's Hall of Fame, the McElroys won 8-2 marking the first time a local team had ever defeated a major league club. A month later Manager Mick Stambaugh's Furniture Men, as the McElroys were sometimes called, beat the Pittsburgh Pirates 7-5 before a huge crowd at Idora.

In addition to the occasional visits by major league clubs, Idora became a frequent stop for teams in the Negro Leagues. African Americans were moving from the South to Youngstown in increasing numbers to work in the steel mills, and they also patronized Idora Park. In September when the McElroys beat Sell Hall's American Giants 17-8, African Americans made up half of the record crowd of three thousand fans.

When the baseball season was over, football games were staged at Idora. One that stirred great interest was a gridiron clash between St. Edwards and the Youngstown Patricians on November 21, 1920. The *Vindicator* declared that only the annual high school matchup between Rayen and South drew more interest than this contest between the Saints and the Pats.

Youngstown's population grew from 79,000 in 1910 to 132,358 in 1920 making it the fiftieth largest city in the United States. Idora's growth in the 1920s would continue to mirror the city's growing importance. In a little more than two decades, the south side of the city had evolved from a rural, isolated area with few residents to a rapidly expanding community with ten public schools, a high school, and hundreds of new homes. Idora Park played a substantial role in this development. It was the dominant amusement park in Youngstown and the surrounding area and competed directly with parks in Akron, Canton, Cleveland, and Pittsburgh.

But its greatest years were yet to come.

By 1920 Idora Park had expanded significantly from its modest beginnings in 1899.
GEORGE SIESSEL COLLECTION

1921 - 1930

4 BILLINGS TAKES CHARGE

The 1921 season was a milestone in Idora's history for it marked the arrival of Rex Billings as Idora's new manager. Royal Platt, who had served in that capacity since 1911, resigned to devote his full attention to operating the concessions he owned in the park.

Rex Billings was a native of Trumbull County and had worked for a time with the Warner Brothers in New Castle, Pennsylvania, before they went to Hollywood. He studied law briefly, became a general claims agent for the Reading Transit and Light Company, and worked at Carsonia Park in Reading, Pennsylvania. He later became Chief Claims Agent for the Pennsylvania-Ohio Power and Light Company before his assignment to manage Idora. Billings was a talented and tireless promoter who would guide the park during its greatest period of expansion. Before he left Idora, he would become one of the stars of the amusement park industry.

Upon assuming the job as manager, Billings announced the changes and improvements for the 1921 season. Roller skating moved to the building previously used as a dining hall. A new lunch room was constructed on the midway next to the photographer's studio. Among the new midway attractions were a pig slide and a water rifle range that replaced the old shooting gallery. Patrons of the dance pavilion would find a new feature. Light was reflected from two spheres covered by a mosaic of mirrors. "This will be the *Myriascope*," explained the *Vindicator*, "something brand new to this section of the country. Two have been installed so that at each end of the hall will be a huge revolving globe upon which two spotlights play, the scintillations of the lights being thrown into all parts of the floor and hall by a myriad of mirrors. Changes of color will add to the beauty of the effect, which generally is that of dancers whirling through a snowstorm." Boyle's Orchestra, which had provided the dance music since 1908, moved to the Casino Theater to provide accompaniment for productions of the Horne Stock Company. A new dance orchestra, Shulansky's Symphonic Syncopators, led by Ben Shulansky, was engaged for the dance pavilion. In the 1920s dancing became much more important to Idora. Manager Billings advised that no "indecorous" dances such as the shimmy or cheek-to-cheek would be permitted in the park.

Billings, although he worked for the trolley company, realized that the role of the automobile was increasing and had the huge parking lot next to the ballroom

People flocked to Idora Park in the 1920s.
MAHONING VALLEY HISTORICAL SOCIETY

Rex Billings, Idora's manager from 1921 through 1930.
CHARLES J. JACQUES, JR. COLLECTION

The street leading to Idora's south entrance was named for Rex Billings.
CHARLES J. JACQUES, JR. COLLECTION

covered with cinders so rain would not turn it into a mudhole. Billings also added a fully equipped playground for the younger children, an early version of Kiddieland. The design was based on ideas brought back to Youngstown by Henry Butler, who observed such a playground near the Eiffel Tower when his wartime duties took him to Paris. This playground was located on the hillside next to the theater.

For the July 4th festivities that year, Paul Rossi of the New Castle Fireworks Company was engaged to provide the pyrotechnical displays. Rossi announced that the show would incorporate some features he acquired as a result of his war experience in Europe. More than thirty thousand people came to the park to see the fireworks and other holiday events,

1921 - 1930

Lillian Desmonde first appeared on the Idora stage in 1920.
MAHONING VALLEY HISTORICAL SOCIETY

Charlie Deibel became a part owner of Idora in 1924.
DR. RICHARD MURRAY COLLECTION

the largest crowd ever to attend the park. The local press announced that "The roads surrounding the park were jammed with automobiles and the congestion was the worst ever known on these roads." A boxing match was also scheduled for the Fourth at Idora, and semi-pro teams regularly played on the Idora baseball field. The McElroys, Youngstown's top semi-pro baseball club, again staged some memorable contests. The Boston Red Sox visited Idora in May and beat the local team 7-4.

Also attracting crowds to Idora that summer of 1921 was Madame Stella Jaeger, an aeronaut, who ascended in a balloon and returned to earth by means of a triple parachute jump. After reaching sufficient height the woman would make the first jump, then cut from her first parachute to a second, and then a third. The landings provided unexpected thrills. On one jump Jaeger landed high in a tree and had to be rescued by the city fire department's hook and ladder company. On another jump she landed in a tomato patch "damaging the ripening crop to such an extent," noted a reporter, "that the park management was forced to settle for the loss." The publicity for such events was well worth the cost.

The July 4th fireworks had proved such a hit that Billings engaged the company to stage additional displays on Saturday nights in August. The spectacle, drawing upon war research in explosives, was constructed around the theme of "The Battle of Chateau-Thierry."

One of Rex Billings' chief goals was to bring more picnic business to Idora, and the largest of his first season as manager was the Youngstown Retail Grocers and Meat Dealers picnic held August 10, 1921. Between 20,000 and 25,000 attended. Ten thousand roast beef sandwiches were distributed with free milk and coffee, and forty-eight thousand tickets were scattered to the crowd. One hundred tickets contained coupons for free groceries. Perhaps it was at this picnic that Rex Billings met Charlie Deibel, a prominent Youngstown area meat dealer, who in three years would become a part owner of the park with Billings.

Idora's owners, the Pennsylvania-Ohio Power and Light Company, also owned and operated Cascade Park, an amusement park in New Castle, Pennsylvania. In August a special streetcar took the Idora employees to Cascade Park for their annual outing, which featured athletic contests and a dance contest. The Idora workers presented Billings with an electric lamp and an ornamental basket. A week later the Cascade Park employees came to Idora for their annual picnic.

For Labor Day the park again staged fireworks and boxing exhibitions, and the Horne Stock Company added additional performances. Lillian Desmonde remained the leading lady. Labor Day marked the end of the season, but the ballroom remained open for the annual Harvest Moon dances. Boyle's Orchestra moved back into the dance pavilion to provide music, and the dances, which ran every night except Mondays, proved so popular that the ballroom season was extended until mid-October.

Billings was interested in finding uses for the park facilities in the off season. In October came an announcement that the Idora Skating Rink had been temporarily converted to a movie studio. A group of local businessmen had formed The Buckeye Pictures Company and had hired a group of men with photoplay experience to produce a series of moving pictures. At least one movie, a one-reel comedy called *Billy B. Wise*, was appar-

ently produced, but no record of that film or subsequent productions appears to exist.

Shortly after the close of the season, Idora Park lost one of its founders. Harry G. Hamilton, who died on October 8, 1921, at the age of 56, had helped create the Park & Falls Street Railway Company and had been responsible more than any other person for the establishment of an amusement park at the end of the trolley line. The *Vindicator* said Hamilton "was almost solely responsible for the founding of East Youngstown and practically the entire South Side." That claim may have been an exaggeration, but it was a fitting tribute to Hamilton's role in Youngstown's growth. By the time Hamilton died, half of the city's growing population resided south of the Mahoning River.

Three attractions that would become enduring favorites at Idora were introduced in 1922: a new carousel, a fun house, and the Dodgems. These three in one form or another would be mainstays of the upper midway for the next sixty years. Management claimed it was spending more than $100,000 on the park for the 1922 season.

The merry-go-round was built by the Philadelphia Toboggan Company of Philadelphia, Pennsylvania, which had constructed the Panama Canal for the park. The carousel was designated #61 by PTC. It had forty-eight horses and two chariots. Carved on the side of one chariot was a woman who cradles a cherub on her lap and holds a garland of roses above

The carousel was built by the Philadelphia Toboggan Company in 1922.
CHARLES J. JACQUES, JR. COLLECTION

The new carousel was installed in the old carousel building.
CHARLES J. JACQUES, JR. COLLECTION

41

1921 - 1930

her flowing tresses. On the front panel another cherub plays a flute. The other chariot displayed a patriotic theme with a design developed by PTC during World War I. The figure of Columbia or Miss Liberty sits with her left hand outstretched and her right hand holding a laurel branch. The American flag is draped around her shoulders. On the front panel of the chariot is a magnificently carved American eagle.

The new carousel was manufactured at Philadelphia Toboggan Company's Germantown factory between January and March of 1922. Gustav Weiss, PTC's head painter, was paid $171.50 to paint the 16 first-row horses, the 16 second-row horses, and the 16 third-row horses. He also created a design for the rim, shaft board, and drop boards of the carousel. To complete the decorations, eighteen beveled mirrors from Benjamin H. Shoemaker of Philadelphia and a #27 fog bell from Bevini Bros. Manufacturing Company were purchased. Music was provided by a Gebruder Bruder band organ, Model 107, 52 keyless. In front of the band organ was a decorative facade.

The ride cost $11,892.11 to build but was carried on the company's books at $16,000. The Philadelphia Toboggan Company retained a half interest in the carousel and sold the other half to the Youngstown Carrousel Company, a new organization of investors that included several executives of PTC. This newly incorporated carousel company also purchased for $1,000 Idora's 1911 Dentzel carousel and moved it to the carousel building in Cascade Park, New Castle, Pennsylvania, which it purchased from Penn-Ohio Power. The Youngstown Carrousel Company operated the carousels at Idora and Cascade Park for the next decade.

T. B. Duffy was sent to Idora by the Philadelphia Toboggan Company to help install the carousel in the existing building that had been erected earlier by T. M. Harton. Duffy was paid $5.00 a day for five days' work on the Idora carousel and the carousel at Cascade Park in New Castle, Pennsylvania. PTC #61 became an important part of any trip to Idora and remained in Idora Park until 1984 when the park closed and the carousel was auctioned off.

The Fun House was one of the costliest features yet constructed at the park. It was designed by one of the greatest amusement park engineers, John A. Miller of Homewood, Illinois, and constructed by the Philadelphia Toboggan Company. Henry B. Auchy, president of PTC, sent H. S. Smith to supervise the construction of the "Youngstown Fun House," as PTC referred to the structure in Idora Park.

As opening day neared, David Jenkins, PTC's manager of rides at Idora and Cascade Park, wrote to Auchy and asked, "What has been done as to a name for this place? Palace of Fun or Colosseum are both good. But would rather have you decide." For a while the building was named All For Fun, but most park visitors simply called it the Fun House.

The Fun House was built at the northern end of the park near the bowling alley in a space formerly used as a pony track. According to the *Vindicator*, the many mirth-provoking devices included "'Roulette wheels,' 'social whirls,' camel back 'bumps,' trick stairways, a slide which is declared by the engineers employed on the construction to be the best in the United States, 'cake walks,' 'turkey trots,' shifting floors, side rockers, wind devices, and innumerable other novelties." The Fun House cost

Idora's new Fun House (left) and Circle Swing with wooden airplanes (right).
CHARLES J. JACQUES, JR. COLLECTION

$23,329.39 to build, but in its first year of operation it returned a profit of only $540.

The Dodgems were also built at the northern end of the park between the Fun House and the bowling alley. In an era when many families were buying their first car, the Dodgem bumper cars gave even the youngsters a chance to drive.

A new pony track was built near the children's playground, and the dance pavilion was remodeled. The orchestra, formerly located in the balcony, was moved to a platform in the center of the dance floor, and sounding boards were placed above the orchestra to evenly distribute the sound. The Premier Orchestra of Chicago conducted by Verne Ricketts was engaged as the "house" orchestra to provide dance music for the whole season. The James Burtis Players were signed to provide summer stock, replacing the Horne Stock Company, which after five seasons at Idora moved to the Hippodrome in downtown Youngstown.

Manager Billings continued his policy of bringing top boxing matches to Idora. For the Decoration Day weekend, Carl Tremaine of Cleveland battled Phil O'Dowd of Columbus at the Idora ball field for the state bantamweight title. A welterweight bout later in the summer created a furor. A local boxer Jimmy Jones won easily when his opponent displayed few skills except the ability to fight dirty. Sportswriter Frank B. Ward called the performance "the poorest exhibition of fistic art ever displayed in this city," and the mismatch prompted Youngstown's mayor William Reese to ban boxing not only at Idora but in the whole city until regulations could be established and enforced. However, the ban was lifted temporarily the following week to allow local lightweight Tony Zill to fight at Idora in a show sponsored by the American Legion.

Although African Americans were normally excluded from the dance pavilion, the Colored Masons of Ohio held their picnic and dance at Idora, and over ten thousand African Americans came to Idora for the day. Part of the festivities included an exhibition baseball game played by the Homestead Grays, a team from the Pittsburgh area. The Grays were one of the best known black baseball teams, and they would return many times to Idora over the next two decades.

The end of the season was given over to Veterans Week, a celebration reunion of World War I veterans and other servicemen in the Mahoning Valley sponsored by the American Legion. Special activities were scheduled for each day, and a sham battle with military fireworks was presented nightly. Other activities included dancing, free acrobatic acts on the midway, and nightly screenings of *Flashes of Action*, motion pictures of the American Expeditionary Force in combat.

For the 1923 season manager Rex Billings added thirteen hundred new trees, shrubs, and flowering plants and adopted the advertising slogan "Beautiful Idora Park." He also continued to add new attractions. The Panama Canal ride was re-themed and became the Wizard of Oz. The ride still carried patrons through a winding tunnel in gondolas, but now the darkness was broken by scenic representations from Frank Baum's popular story. Major repairs were needed after a rotten section of the channel gave way, which emptied the ride of its water, and the attraction was forced to close for three weeks early in the season. The Circle Swing was replaced by a much larger Giant Aeroplane Swing, and the Caterpillar made its first appearance at Idora. Both the rides were purchased from Harry Traver and were manufac-

1921 - 1930

The Caterpillar, an early flat ride, was purchased in 1923.
RICK SHALE COLLECTION

In the 1920s people often brought picnic lunches to Idora.
RICK SHALE COLLECTION

tured by Traver Engineering of Beaver Falls, Pennsylvania. On the Caterpillar passengers rode a circular, undulating track. Midway through the ride a canvas covering enveloped the cars. The *Youngstown Telegram* reported that this thrill ride looked like a large caterpillar, "but it is what happens after the cover descends that makes for the thrill."

Billings also renovated the children's area on the hill, adding a new double slide, see-saws, sand piles, and a miniature merry-go-round. Helen Nolan, the daughter of park police sergeant James Nolan was hired as playground supervisor, and she provided a story hour each afternoon and organized games for the young ones.

Summer stock remained very popular, and in 1923 the Burns-Kasper Company provided the theatrical entertainment. Nat Burns was no stranger to Youngstown audiences, who had seen the actor-director at the Hippodrome as well as Idora in previous seasons. Edwin H. Kasper served as leading man, and the supporting cast included a Youngstown girl, Catherine Hitchings, whom Burns had discovered the previous summer. Manager Rex Billings found Hitchings so attractive that he married her.

Idora's ownership ties to the trolley industry ended in April 1924, when the Pennsylvania-Ohio Power and Light Company sold the park to the Idora Amusement Company. The new company was composed of well-known Youngstown businessmen, and the transaction meant that for the first time in its history Idora was completely under local control. The new owners consisted of Charles Deibel, a grocer and meat dealer, who was elected president; Rex Billings, vice-president and general manager; Adolph H. Heller, secretary; and Thomas H. Murray, Jr., treasurer. Murray, who was Deibel's son-in-law, and Heller were prominent local contractors who had constructed some of Youngstown's most important buildings. The new board of directors was composed of the four officers plus Attorney John W. Ford. Billings, in addition to becoming a co-owner, remained manager of Idora and also served as president of the Springbrook Park Company in South Bend, Indiana, and secretary-treasurer of the Meyers Lake Miniature Railway Company in Canton, Ohio. He announced that under the new ownership Idora would maintain the same high standards and also revealed that the park would construct a $100,000 swimming pool.

Idora had many rides and attractions but no swimming facilities. This put Idora at a distinct disadvantage because many of its competitors such as Cascade Park in New Castle, Pennsylvania; Craig Beach Park at Lake Milton, Ohio's Conneaut Lake Park in Conneaut, Ohio; and Lake Brady Park near Ravenna, Ohio, offered swimming and boating.

The decision to build a pool was a timely one. Youngstown had only two municipal pools, and the city's population was growing rapidly, increasing 67 percent over the previous decade. In 1921 the State Board of Health had recommended that swimming be discontinued in the lakes in nearby Mill Creek Park. To finance the new swimming facility, Rex Billings persuaded several prominent local businessmen to invest in the project, and a new corporation was formed.

The new pool was built by the Heller-Murray Construction Company and was located in the northeast section of the park adjacent to the midway near the old skating rink. The oval pool measured 210 by 160 feet and was surrounded by a 20-foot-wide white sand beach. Lighting allowed night swimming. The pool measured 10 feet, 6 inches at its deepest point with a diving tower in the center. A semi-circular amphitheater done in a Georgian Revival style formed a backdrop for the pool and housed the dressing rooms and filtration plant. Numbered hangers and lockers were provided to check clothing and belongings. This structure was designed by Alexander Lynch of New Haven, Connecticut, who was considered one of the country's leading natatorium engineers.

Admission was 50 cents for those who had their own suit and 75 cents for those who needed to rent a wool swimsuit. The pool also had an electric sanitary laundry that was capable of drying five hundred suits in twenty minutes. Management stressed safety and hygiene. The million and a half gallons of water in the pool were constantly circulated and changed every twenty hours. Brightly colored buoys marked the deep water, and a special section of the pool was set aside for children.

Although the pool was within the

Playbill for the Tarona Players, a stock company that performed at Idora.
RICK SHALE COLLECTION

Bathing beauties on the sand beach in front of the park's bathhouse.
RICK SHALE COLLECTION

1921 - 1930

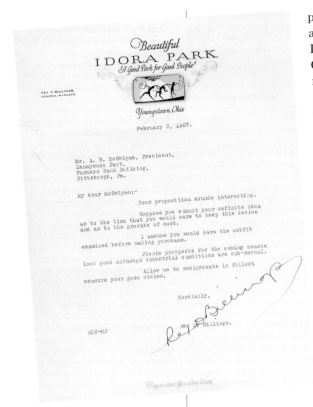

park, it was built and operated by the Idora Natatorium Company, whose directors included: L. B. McKelvey, president; Benjamin Agler, secretary; Philip Schaff, treasurer; Emil Renner, general manager; and Thomas Barrett, pool manager. The pool opened on Saturday afternoon, June 14, 1924, and was an immediate hit. Kennywood Park in Pittsburgh opened a swimming pool the following season, and frequent correspondence between Rex Billings and the Kennywood owners indicates that the pools were a major help in soliciting picnic business.

The pool was also used to showcase daredevil acts. In 1926, for example, Idora booked Bench Bentum, a champion high and fancy diver. One of her stunts was diving from a height of fifty feet into a special tank holding just four feet of water. That same summer a bathing beauty contest was held at the pool as part of the Timken Bearing Company annual picnic.

In 1924 the park also advertised a new $75,000 coaster, but it was really the old Dip-the-Dips that had been remodeled into an out-and-back coaster with a sixty-three-foot first drop. This "new" coaster was named the Jack Rabbit. Edward Vettel of the T. M. Harton Company did the reworking of the coaster.

Company picnics were still the bread and butter of the park business, and the new pool helped Billings greatly increase the picnic bookings. To serve those who did not bring a picnic basket, a cafeteria was added to the midway, and a new well provided additional drinking fountains. The Mysterious Knockout and a miniature auto race track for the kids were added.

Verne Ricketts' Orchestra was again engaged for the ballroom, and the Lillian Desmonde Players were hired to provide theatrical entertainment. Desmonde had won many fans when she starred for two seasons with the Horne Stock Company, and she now returned to Idora with her own stock company.

Baseball continued to draw crowds, and fans could count on high quality semi-pro competition and exhibition

James Dimmick's Sunnybrook Orchestra served as the house band in the mid 1920s.
MAHONING VALLEY HISTORICAL SOCIETY

games with teams from the major leagues, Negro Leagues, and other barnstorming organizations. The Cuban Giants from Brooklyn came in 1924, as did one of the most unusual teams ever to visit Idora. The House of David traced its origins to a Hebrew communal colony founded in 1903 in Benton Harbor, Michigan. By the 1920s several House of David teams were touring the country playing exhibition baseball. The players all wore beards and shoulder-length hair. The *Vindicator* explained that "The players appear on the field before the game with their hair down, but before the play starts, they tuck their long locks under their caps." Nearly three thousand fans turned out at Idora to watch the local General Tires team edge the House of David 3-2.

The Ku Klux Klan experienced a resurgence in the Youngstown area in the early 1920s and had captured a number of political offices in 1923 including mayor of Youngstown and six of the seven City Council positions. In the summer of 1924 the Klan held a picnic at Idora that drew seven thousand people. Hundreds of American flags were displayed. The *Vindicator* reported that "The Red Robed Riders were on the scene and had a special tent and politicians were as thick as a swarm of bees in an orchard." The Klan newspaper *The Citizen* praised Idora in an editorial, noting that "Idora is more of a summer home and less of an institution than other places." In October the Klan sponsored a circus at Idora.

One of Rex Billings' most popular and lasting innovations was the 3-cent kiddies' day promotion. During the summer the park would run a number of kiddies' days. Children under sixteen received free streetcar transportation to Idora during off-peak hours. Rides were specially priced at 3 cents except for the Fun House, theater, and swimming pool where the admission was 10 cents. These bargain days were often sponsored by a local company such as the Holland Bread or Youngstown Sanitary Milk Company as a promotion. For the Holland Bread Kiddies' Day on July 1, 1925, the youngsters were encouraged to save Certified or Butter Krust bread wrappers, which were needed to qualify for the 3-cent discount ticket.

Idora's baseball field hosted many major league exhibitions in the 1920s.
RICK SHALE COLLECTION

The Cincinnati Reds, led by two-time batting champion Edd Roush, played an exhibition game at Idora in 1925 against Youngstown's top semi-pro team, now sponsored by General Tires. The locals lost to the Reds but redeemed themselves by beating the Philadelphia Phillies, another National League team. When the Phillies returned later in the season, the local team beat them again. General Tires also bested the Carnegie Elks, a semi-pro team from Pennsylvania led by player-manager Honus Wagner, the retired Pittsburgh Pirate and future Hall of Famer.

The 1926 season saw the introduction of Skee Ball and 1001 Troubles, a walk-through attraction from the Charles Browning Amusement Company that was found in more than twenty-five amusement parks. A newer model Whip replaced the old one, and a larger Airplane Swing was installed. The kiddie auto race track was enlarged, and the theater was given a new entrance. A Dangler or chain swing was imported from Europe.

Because African American baseball players were banned from the major leagues, sports fans regularly speculated on how the Negro League teams would fare against the big league clubs. In 1926 an aggregation of American League All-Stars scheduled a three-game exhibition against the Homestead Grays. The first was played at Idora Park on October 4th, and the final two games were held in

Lillian Desmonde, Idora's premiere actress of the 1920s.
MAHONING VALLEY HISTORICAL SOCIETY

1921 - 1930

Rex Billings' children in the Indian village at Idora in 1926.
DOLLY BILLINGS MILLER COLLECTION

A bathing beauty contest at Idora's natatorium in 1926.
MAHONING VALLEY HISTORICAL SOCIETY

Pittsburgh. Leading the All-Stars was the Detroit Tigers' Heinie Manush, who would win the batting crown that year with a .378 average. Sportswriter Lawrence Stolle wrote, "The fans were more numerous than rats in Hamelin. They dotted the bleachers, perched on the fence, sat in the outfield, stood on the sidelines, and occupied every available space on the Jack Rabbit." The record crowd of eight thousand saw the American League All-Stars win 11-6 in ten innings. Cleveland Indians first baseman George Burns had three doubles and two singles, and Manush tripled and doubled to pace the major leaguers. Management rebuilt the ball field for the following season with five hundred tons of dirt and a new drainage system to keep the ballpark up to the standard needed for such big games.

The 1927 season began with a record Memorial Day crowd of more than thirty thousand. Visitors discovered eighty-five hundred feet of new sidewalk built along the midway. At the boxing match staged on the holiday evening, Manager Billings announced that more cars had been parked in the parking lot than ever before. Jimmy Dimmick's Sunnybrook Orchestra provided dance music as it had in 1926, and the Lillian Desmonde Players began their fourth season at the theater.

If people remember seeing a play at Idora Park, the chances are good that it starred Lillian Desmonde. By 1927 she had presented nearly one hundred plays to Youngstown audiences. On September 1, 1927, she gave her one-thousandth local performance, and a capacity audience at the Idora theater marked the occasion with a tribute. At the conclusion of the second act, Jimmy Dimmick's Sunnybrook Orchestra marched into the theater playing "Hail, Hail, the Gang's All Here." Miss Desmonde thanked the crowd for its loyalty over the past several seasons. The *Youngstown Telegram* reported that the band then "played 'Auld Lang Syne' and a veritable garden of bouquets was passed over the footlights."

Idora's dance policy in those days is disclosed in a letter sent by Rex Billings to Brady McSwigan, president of Kennywood Park, on May 11, 1927:

>*We use park plan dancing and this season will charge a 15 cent admission to the pavilion in addition to the per dance fee. We used a 10-cent gate in 1926 with very good results as to revenue and the elimination of undesirables from the promenade.*
>
>*We use, in addition to our general admission personnel, a man on each gate which opens on to the floor proper. In our case, this means 7 men when we are in full operation at night but only 2 or 3 in the afternoon. A dance hall of our size requires two ticket sellers in addition. We are favorably inclined toward the use of ticket chopper boxes which are placed in the dance floor at the middle of each entrance until the patrons are all on the floor at which time the boxes are removed to one side. Our gate attendants are uniformed.*
>
>*We get 10 cents per dance and sell 14 tickets for $1.00 at Idora Park, ... In view of the price we charge we give a rather long dance. A Waltz will run 5 minutes and other numbers from 4 to 4 1/2 minutes. We use a fake encore. By this, I mean that halfway through the number we stop for 3 or 4 beats. This creates the impression of a longer dance and affords desirable relaxation to the dancers.*

Dance band at Idora Park.
RICK SHALE COLLECTION

We often clear our floor during rush business in 50 seconds. This is accomplished by using all of the entrances as exits and taking out the four corners of the railing that surrounds the floor and substituting velvet ropes. We do not rope the people from the floor as this has always seemed objectionable to me and too much like herding cattle.

"Bigger and Better Than Ever" was the slogan for the 1928 season. Hy Steed and his Commodores, a protégé of Jimmy Dimmick, opened the season in the dance pavilion, and popular Lillian Desmonde again presented summer stock.

The Tilt-a-Whirl, a flat ride, was added to the park in 1928 at a cost of $7,000. It was built by the Sellner Manufacturing Company of Faribault, Minnesota, which advertised the attraction as "Built of Steel, runs like a top, has a whirlwind of sensation — that's the Tilt-a-Whirl!" This ride proved to have enduring popularity, and one model or another of the Tilt-a-Whirl spun Idora patrons for the next fifty-six years until the park closed.

Monkey Island, the most popular animal attraction in the park's history, premiered in 1928 when over fifty monkeys took up residence in Idora. Billings also imported a herd of Alaskan reindeer. A camel was promised, but it was quarantined in New York and did not arrive for opening day.

In addition to the Tilt-a-Whirl and Monkey Island, Idora in 1928 offered the following attractions: dance pavilion, restaurant, theater, swimming pool, giant aeroplane swing, Jack Rabbit roller coaster, PTC #61 merry-go-round, Whip, Fun House, Gondola Glide, Firefly roller coaster, Skee-Ball alleys, photo gallery, Auto Speedway, kiddie aeroplane swing, Ferris wheel, Wizard of Oz, 1001 Troubles, kiddie swan ride, Skooter, Dangler, penny arcade, and midway novelties.

Idora's carousel, PTC #61, continued to be owned and operated by the Youngstown Carrousel Company. In 1928 the carousel earned a $2,100.32 profit after paying $1,657.11 in rent to Idora Park. (By comparison, the Youngstown Carrousel Company's other carousel at Cascade Park in New Castle earned only $300 after paying $707.18 in rent.)

Lillian Desmonde gave over one thousand performances at Idora's theater.
MAHONING VALLEY HISTORICAL SOCIETY

Parking facilities for automobiles had to be expanded in the 1920s.
RICK SHALE COLLECTION

1921 - 1930

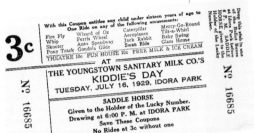

The monkeys proved such an attraction that for the 1929 season the park added a kiddie zoo including miniature circus wagons. The dance pavilion was completely redecorated, and Ace Brigode and his Fourteen Virginians were booked for the season. A new feature for 1929 was "miracle music." "Where does it come from?" and "What causes it?" were the two most frequent questions, or so claimed the ads. The "miracle" was achieved by stringing speakers throughout the park and playing amplified music on the grounds.

At the turn of the century many parks had three or four band organs on different rides and in the restaurant and dance pavilion. Sometimes the band organ would alternate with live musicians. By the late 1920s amplified music was slowly replacing the mechanical organs in amusement parks although band organs remained on carousels.

The Pittsburgh Pirates, led by future Hall of Famer Lloyd Waner, made one of their periodic visits and trimmed the Youngstown Oaklands 9-5. Two weeks later the Brooklyn Dodgers visited Idora, and this time the Oaklands prevailed. The game was held to honor Youngstown's only representative in the major leagues, Billy Rhiel, who played second base for the Dodgers. Rhiel was given a check for $500 from his local booster club. On hand to throw out the first pitch was Jim Corbett, former heavyweight boxing champ from 1892 to 1897.

Rex Billings, in his ninth year as manager and sixth as part owner, was honored, as few amusement park owners have ever been: on June 17, 1929, Youngstown's City Council officially adopted an ordinance designating the name of the street leading to Idora's south entrance as Billingsgate. Within two years Billings would leave Youngstown to manage Coney Island's Luna Park in New York City, but the street named remained. Today, seven decades later, Billingsgate still remains as a monument to the golden age of Idora Park under Rex Billings' leadership.

Ace Brigode's Orchestra provided dance music for the 1929 and 1930 seasons.
RICK SHALE COLLECTION

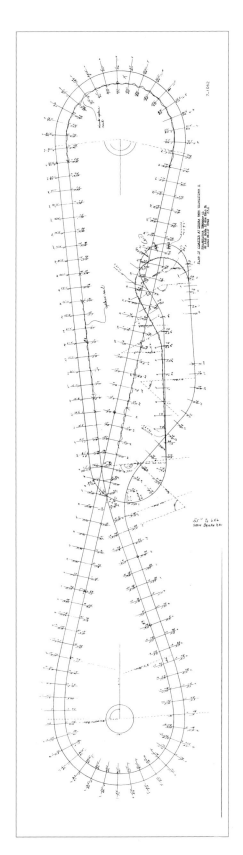

Wildcat blueprint.
COURTESY OF THE HISTORIC AMUSEMENT FOUNDATION

The Wildcat (above and below) under construction during the winter of 1929-30.
CHARLES J. JACQUES, JR. COLLECTION

The 1930 season was another of those milestones in Idora's history. A new slogan "Now–A Million Dollar Park" reflected nearly $200,000 worth of improvements that greeted visitors that summer. A new roller coaster called the Wildcat replaced the old Firefly, and a new water ride called the Rapids replaced the old Philadelphia Toboggan Company red mill, which had operated under the names Panama Canal and the Wizard of Oz. The midway was enlarged by five hundred feet, and a new dark ride called the Pretzel was installed. Ace Brigode and his Fourteen Virginians were booked for a return engagement.

Billings continued to capitalize on the public's love of sports and added regulation archery, which was enjoying a nationwide boom. Another fad sweeping the country in 1930 was miniature golf. Idora's ads urged people to forget their troubles and try The 19th Hole: "Come and see the game that has taken Florida and California society by storm. The game that has made the movie stars rush from their dressing rooms. The greatest game ever invented for those suffering from the bite of the golf bug." The game was so new to Youngstowners that the *Vindicator* felt obliged to explain "This course is played entirely with a putter."

The Rapids, which occupied approximately the same site as the old Firefly coaster, was a much larger and improved version of the old Panama Canal ride also built by the Philadelphia To-

1921 - 1930

The Wildcat was designed by Herbert Schmeck of the Philadelphia Toboggan Company.
CHARLES J. JACQUES, JR. COLLECTION

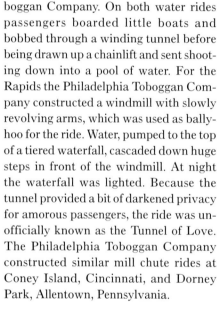

In 1930 the midway was redesigned to make room for the Wildcat and Rapids.
CHARLES J. JACQUES, JR. COLLECTION

boggan Company. On both water rides passengers boarded little boats and bobbed through a winding tunnel before being drawn up a chainlift and sent shooting down into a pool of water. For the Rapids the Philadelphia Toboggan Company constructed a windmill with slowly revolving arms, which was used as ballyhoo for the ride. Water, pumped to the top of a tiered waterfall, cascaded down huge steps in front of the windmill. At night the waterfall was lighted. Because the tunnel provided a bit of darkened privacy for amorous passengers, the ride was unofficially known as the Tunnel of Love. The Philadelphia Toboggan Company constructed similar mill chute rides at Coney Island, Cincinnati, and Dorney Park, Allentown, Pennsylvania.

To put the finishing touches on the Old Mill and other attractions, Billings hired Charles Edwards, a scenic artist, who had done work for Youngstown's Hippodrome Theater. Edwards was an itinerant scenic artist who traveled from job to job painting in theaters in the summer and amusement parks in the spring and fall. At Idora he painted the scenery sheds in the new Rapids and added scenic effects to the cascading waterfall in front of the mill. He also worked on the Fun House and the new Pretzel dark ride and even designed a northern lights effect for the Frozen Custard stand.

The Wildcat (PTC Coaster #83) became a lasting landmark of the park. This coaster was constructed in the fall of 1929 by the Philadelphia Toboggan Company and was ready for opening day of the 1930 season. The old Firefly had been owned by a concessionaire, but the new Wildcat was owned by the park. The minutes of the January 2, 1929, meeting of the Philadelphia Toboggan Company noted that Idora ardently desired a superior, first-class coaster: "The Idora Park coaster and Mill situation has been held up by the release of the old coaster site which is to be occupied with the Mill, and so far Mr. Billings has not been able to secure this release. He has been hoping to get it almost any day now, and says that we are to have the coaster order when he does get it." By fall the situation had improved, and the PTC minutes of October 21, 1929, recorded, "we have a coaster and Mill Chutes order for Idora Park, Youngstown — working on the coaster now, the Mill Chutes will probably not be built until Spring, both of these are under a 'Plans and Equipment' basis." This meant that PTC provided the plans and a first class construction supervisor, George J. Baker. The company also manufactured the coaster cars and provided other coaster hardware.

George P. Smith Jr., general manager of PTC, wrote Brady McSwigan of Kennywood Park on October 24, 1929: "Yes, I do think Rex Billings is going to have a wonderful coaster. The Mill Chutes we are going to build him in the spring also will be an added attraction to his park, and they should both be of help to him in building up his business." With his subtle boasting, Smith was reminding McSwigan that such construction would have to be matched if Kennywood expected to remain competitive.

The Wildcat was designed by PTC's greatest coaster engineer, Herbert Schmeck, who designed almost all PTC coasters from 1924 to 1954. By 1930 Schmeck had developed a twister coaster that employed an "aeroplane curve" for its first drop and a descending curve for its second drop. Idora's Wildcat was one of the finest examples of Schmeck's twister coaster. The Wildcat occupied a small area, and yet with its tunnels and banked curves it was one of the greatest coasters built in the 1920s.

A June 8, 1930, *Vindicator* rotogravure picture shows *Vindicator* reporter Ella Kerber Resch, band leader Ace Brigode, and young Ed Conner, who is credited with winning the contest to name the new coaster. The winner may have simply accepted a company suggestion since the Wildcat was a generic name often used by the Philadelphia Toboggan

The newly opened Rapids and Wildcat as seen from the roof of the ballroom.
CHARLES J. JACQUES, JR. COLLECTION

Ballyhoo for the Rapids included an old windmill and waterfall.
CHARLES J. JACQUES, JR. COLLECTION

1921 - 1930

Original cars on the Wildcat's south turn circa 1930.
CHARLES J. JACQUES, JR. COLLECTION

Company. The company would use that name unless the park owners specifically asked for something else. John Miller used Jack Rabbit; Harry Baker used Whippet; and Herb Schmeck used, when possible, the Wildcat.

Sports fans were treated to a novelty in late July when night baseball made its debut at Idora in a game between two Negro League teams. The Homestead Grays beat the Kansas City Monarchs under a system of portable lights. The Monarchs traveled with a 250-horsepower motor, a 100-watt generator, and a series of telescoping poles that raised the lights fifty feet above the field. The system lit the field sufficiently, but the generators were noisy and the placement of the trucks holding the lights along the first and third base lines limited the field of play.

The Grays returned a month later and beat the local Fosterville Merchants 5-4 in a game filled with arguments. When the Grays' fiery first baseman and future Hall-of-Famer, Oscar Charleston was ejected from the game, he chartered the Jack Rabbit and spent the rest of the game hooting at the local players and the umpires as he traveled over the dips and curves of the coaster that bordered the field.

By 1930 public taste in entertainment was shifting, and summer stock was on the decline. Idora's owners were forced to use profits from the park's more lucrative attractions to make up deficits at the theater. The introduction of sound to motion pictures no doubt had something to do with this shift. The *Vindicator* reported in 1930 that the Lillian Desmonde Players were one of only five dramatic stock companies remaining in the country and one of only two that were playing in amusement parks. In 1929 Lillian Desmonde had taken her company to the Hippodrome in downtown Youngstown, while the Tarona Players had been engaged at Idora, but the policy of having two companies play the same town had been a disaster for both. Her husband and partner in the stock company, Jack Hammond, died in 1930, and Lillian Desmonde performed on a much more limited basis after that.

The summer of 1930 was also Rex Billings' last season as Idora's manager. In early April 1931 Billings left Youngstown for New York to manage Coney Island's famed Luna Park. He retained his financial interest in Idora. *Amusement Park Management*, one of the industry's trade journals, rated Billings as "one of the best of the modern school of entrepreneurs in the park business" and noted that through his efforts Idora had become one of the leading amusement parks in the country.

Charlie Deibel, president of the Idora Amusement Company, assumed the duties of general manager with Edward Gilronan, later a prominent Mahoning County commissioner, serving as assistant manager.

The number of citizens in Youngstown had nearly quadrupled since the turn of the century. The city's population peaked at 170,000 in 1930 and would remain relatively stable for the next three decades. The Great Depression of the 1930s would make it difficult for Idora's owners to match the crowds of the park's early years, but at least the park survived the lean economic times. Most parks would not be able to make that claim. Approximately 900 amusement parks were in operation in the country in 1930; by the end of the decade only 300 remained.

The Wildcat's first drop originally featured an exciting swoop turn.
CHARLES J. JACQUES, JR. COLLECTION

1931 - 1945

5 THE BIG BAND YEARS

The Depression especially hurt picnic bookings. Fewer companies scheduled outings, and parks such as West View, Kennywood, Conneaut Lake, Rocky Springs, Meyers Lake, Summit Beach, and Geauga Lake were fighting for their survival. In order to secure some of the remaining picnics, some parks resorted to "bribing" members of the picnic committees with little gifts and extras, and discounting was widespread.

In 1928 parks across the nation had reported that 40 percent of their gross profits had come from picnics. In 1929 the figure climbed to 48 percent, but in 1930, the first season after the stock market crash, the percentage fell to 24.5. Sixty-three percent of parks polled had seen an increase in bookings in 1929, but only 33 percent saw their bookings increase in 1930. By 1931 84 percent of the parks in the country reported a drop in receipts.

A report circulated that Idora would soon close, but the owners quickly denied this. "There is no truth to the report," said Eddie Gilronan, assistant manager. As proof he released a list of two dozen picnics already booked for the 1931 season. Idora survived the worst years of the Great Depression because of strong ownership, the best ballroom in the area, a top coaster and other thrill rides, and a solid schedule of industrial picnics.

The ballroom underwent another remodeling, this time supervised by Leo Cathé of Cleveland, a former art director for Paramount and Pathé. Chic Scoggins and his Orchestra, recording artists on the Brunswick label, provided the dance music for the 1931 season.

The Carlton Brickert Players were booked for the theater, and for their first production, *Thin Ice*, silent film star Francis X. Bushman, was signed as the guest star. Prices were set at 75 cents for the evenings and 35 cents for the matinees. The stock company followed with *Strictly Dishonorable* but apparently did not last the season. By mid-July The Mary-Jane Lane Stock Company was in residence. Ticket prices were dropped to 50 cents for evenings and 25 cents and 10 cents for matinees. The Little German Band, radio stars from Station KDKA in Pittsburgh, also made a guest appearance in July. Plays continued to be presented in Idora's theater, but 1931 marked the end of the tradition of a stock company performing for an entire season.

A new ride was added to capitalize on the popularity of an American hero. Charles Lindbergh had captured the nation's imagination with his 1927 transatlantic flight, and by 1931 Idora had installed the Lindy Loop, which was

Idora Park employees in 1931.
MARCELLA DUFFY COLLECTION

Front, left to right: J. Howard O'Neill, Pat Duffy, Sr., Pat Duffy, Jr. Back: Edward Gilronan.
RICK SHALE COLLECTION

Families arrive at Youngstown's Erie Railroad Station for a company picnic at Idora.
MAHONING VALLEY HISTORICAL SOCIETY

manufactured by Spillman Engineering in Tonawanda, New York.

Professional baseball came to the park in 1931 as Youngstown landed a franchise in the Class C Middle Atlantic League. The Youngstown Buckeyes used Idora as their home field. Youngstown's catcher Babe Phelps batted .408 to win the league batting title. A highlight of the season was an exhibition game with the Cleveland Indians played August 18, 1931. The game was held in honor of Billy Evans, a local man and former *Vindicator* sports writer, who had become a major league umpire and then general manager of the Indians. Evans would eventually be elected to baseball's Hall of Fame. The Indians' center fielder Earl Averill, another future Hall of Famer, hit a home run into the Jack Rabbit, but the Youngstown Buckeyes beat the big leaguers 10 to 7. Bessie Love, star of MGM's Oscar-winning best picture *The Broadway Melody*, attended the game and helped honor Evans.

To keep the customers coming to Idora in those tough economic times, Manager Charlie Deibel announced a 1932 price reduction on several attractions. Parking was 25 cents but included a 10-cent rebate on any purchase in the park, so the actual cost was only 15 cents. The Wildcat and other high-priced rides were reduced to 10 cents. The fees for the merry-go-round and Ferris wheel were decreased to a nickel, and a round of miniature golf was cut to a dime. Free shows on the midway were offered as another inducement. Al Hatch and his trained animals, including dogs, ponies, and monkeys, performed twice daily.

In 1932 the *Vindicator* and the Hi-Y clubs of the Mahoning Valley jointly sponsored the first High School Day and began a tradition that would last for decades. The Hi-Y clubs were for high school boys. Later, the Tri-Hi-Y clubs, which were for girls, joined in the event. The *Vindicator* Hi-Y-Tri-Hi-Y Day

1931 - 1945

The park's swimming pool.
CHARLES J. JACQUES, JR. COLLECTION

Idora Swimming Ticket

This coupon and 20 cents will admit an adult to the Idora Natatorium pool all day, Monday, July 2. The coupon and 12 cents will admit a child. The cash fee will include the tax.

Good Only Monday, July 2nd

Charles Hoover (above) operated the park's photo gallery (right) for many years.
DONALD K. HOOVER COLLECTION

structed at considerable cost a decade earlier, was converted into a new roller skating rink. Other changes included the addition of a new ride called "To Helenback" (the play on words undoubtedly dictated by the proprieties of the times) and a new diving tower for the swimming pool. Pool manager Mike Jennings said that the opening would be the first time in three years that his son would not have the honor of being the season's first swimmer. Five-year-old Mike Jr. was at home with whooping cough.

The Youngstown Buckeyes continued to play at Idora in 1932 but switched from the Class C Middle Atlantic League to the Class B Central League. The Central League folded at the end of the season, and Idora would not have a minor league team again until 1939.

In June the park announced it would hold dances on Sunday, a policy change that drew swift opposition in the form of the following petition sent to the city clerk: "In [sic] behalf of the members of the Women's Christian Temperance Union, we desire to most emphatically protest against the opening of any dance hall in the city of Youngstown on the Sabbath Day and would favor any legislation prohibiting same."

Another policy that surely drew the wrath of the W.C.T.U. was the repeal of Prohibition. Though President Roosevelt did not sign the new law until December 5, 1933, Congress had modified the

usually marked the first day of the season. Idora advertised fifty-two feature attractions including the ballroom "where refined dancing prevails." Freddie Bergin and his Orchestra, which had made a brief appearance in 1931, was booked for the dance season. Bergin's group included a tap dancer, a blues singer, and a trumpet soloist and was regarded as a dance band and vaudeville show rolled into one.

The Fun House, which had been con-

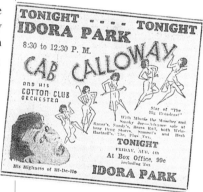

Charlie Deibel and his dog Queenie in one of the park's landscaped gardens.
MARCELLA DUFFY COLLECTION

Volstead Act earlier in 1933 to permit the sale of 3.2 percent beer and wine. The Ohio legislature authorized the sale of beer and wine to begin April 7th, and the Idora management took advantage of the change to create Heidelberg Gardens, a beer garden with an Old World theme. The waitresses dressed as German peasant girls, and the interior had scenic effects painted by a German artist. Heidelberg Gardens was located in the former Casino building in the northwest corner of the park. It became the park's primary eating location, which allowed the cafeteria building across the midway from the Wildcat to be converted into the Penny Arcade.

Red Nichols and his world famous Pennies Orchestra made their first appearance in Youngstown to open Idora's 1933 season, and during intermission of the opening night concert a free fireworks show was presented in the ball field. The crowd was one of the largest in years: "The best attended park sponsored dance on record," claimed Assistant Manager Edward Gilronan. "It seemed like pre-Depression days," said Manager Charles Deibel.

In 1933 Idora shifted from booking a house band for the season to a policy of bringing in name bands. Public taste had shifted from concert bands to dance bands, and the development and growth of the radio industry over the past decade had bestowed celebrity status on many dance orchestras and their leaders. In addition to Red Nichols' appearance, Ben Bernie, Cab Calloway, and Guy Lombardo also were slated to appear. Among the groups playing for Idora's spring prom and party season were the Zack Whyte Band, Jack Denny Band, and Ted Stults and his Carnegie Tartans.

The 1933 season marked the passing of another of Idora's pioneers, Edward Stanley. He had managed Idora Park for the first five years and had been instrumental in establishing Idora's tradition of live theater. *Youngstown*

Idora postcard from the 1930s.
RICHARD L. BOWKER COLLECTION

1931 - 1945

Park employees posed for portraits in 1936.
EDWARD C. LEARNER COLLECTION

The Rapids ride ended with a splashdown in front of the Old Mill and waterfall.
CHARLES J. JACQUES, JR. COLLECTION

Telegram columnist Charlie Leedy recalled that Stanley had once hired him to perform a gun-juggling act at the old Globe Theater on Federal Street and later at Idora Park. In an affectionate eulogy, Leedy wrote of Stanley, "Many people in Youngstown remember him as the original manager of Idora Park and especially for the talks he used to make at each performance, directing attention to the moral tone of the show and urging his hearers to maintain the high standards which the park enjoyed. The Idora Casino shows were of exceptional quality because many of the headliners came to play for Stanley thru [sic] friendship."

Women's baseball teams had been a novelty since the turn of the century, and several Bloomer Girl teams had barnstormed around the country throughout the years. In August the world champion Lena Bloomer Girls of Cleveland came to Idora to play a double-header against two local women's teams. In the first game the Bloomer Girls beat a team of African American All-Stars; in the second, they defeated a white All-Star team.

Idora, like most parks, held off adding major improvements during the first few years of the Depression. But good business at the end of the summer prompted many parks to make plans for a prosperous 1934 season. Early in 1934 Bert Stock replaced Gilronan as Deibel's assistant manager. Stock had eleven years' experience in the orchestra business and most recently had been working for WKBN radio as an announcer and promotions manager. His musical background helped him to book top acts for Idora's ballroom. The turnaround in business as well as Idora's dance band policy is revealed in an April 13, 1934, letter from Stock to Kennywood Park: "We are extremely busy here at Idora, just about like Kennywood and to be frank with you we are away in advance of previous years as to May parties and picnics. The season looks great. We're going out after it. Our plans for the ballroom will be a semi-house band for the season and then possibly bring in a name attraction not more than twice a month."

Stock put his connections with WKBN to good use. The *Vindicator* reported that on May 27th the station would begin "an every evening series of radio broadcasts from the 'Pavillon Moderne.' By remote control WKBN every evening will broadcast the programs of Idora's dance bands." The first broadcast featured Hod Williams and his Orchestra.

Also appearing during the park's opening week was California Frank's Rodeo and Wild West show with bucking broncos, Texas longhorns, and Marie Francis, the world champion horseback rifle and pistol shot. Animals and animal acts continued to be crowd pleasers. Routon's Dog Show and a Rabbit Race Track joined Monkey Island as midway attractions.

The Aut Mori Grotto sponsored a beauty contest at Idora, and Dorothy Moore was chosen as Miss Youngstown over fifteen other contestants including Mary Kosa, who had earlier been named Miss Beautiful Idora to represent the park in the competition.

By June the park announced that a record number of group picnics had been booked. Companies such as Firestone Rubber and Seiberling Tire & Rubber of Akron, Armstrong Cork of Pittsburgh, and Truscon Steel, and organizations like B'nai B'rith, the Mahoning County Teachers, and the Independent Order of Odd Fellows came to Idora for their outings. Nationality days grew increasingly popular, and the Italians, Germans, Scotch, Ukrainians, Slovaks, Croatians, Hungarians, Welsh, Irish, and Russians all held special days at the park.

In 1934 a heating plant was added to the dance pavilion to allow year round dancing. One event held that autumn brought the park considerable publicity. A "Race of Nations" Walkathon was held in the ballroom with $500 to be awarded to the winning couple, $300 to the second couple, and $200 to the third couple. The Depression-era walkathons and dance marathons, says historian Carol Martin, "were an amalgamation of social dance, popular music, theater, and sport. Stunts and sketch material came from vaudeville and the theater; body style and movement were borrowed from vernacular dance; jazz rhythms came from popular music; and from sports came competition, gambling, and the concept of the fan." Such events were not new to the area; in 1923 a Youngstown couple had briefly held the world record for marathon dancing.

Thirty-one couples entered the event at Idora, including fourteen from Youngstown and two from Struthers, and special bleachers for spectators were erected

The pony track was located near the ballroom in the 1930s.
DONALD K. HOOVER COLLECTION

View of the lower midway with the ballroom, Rapids, and Wildcat.
MARCELLA DUFFY COLLECTION

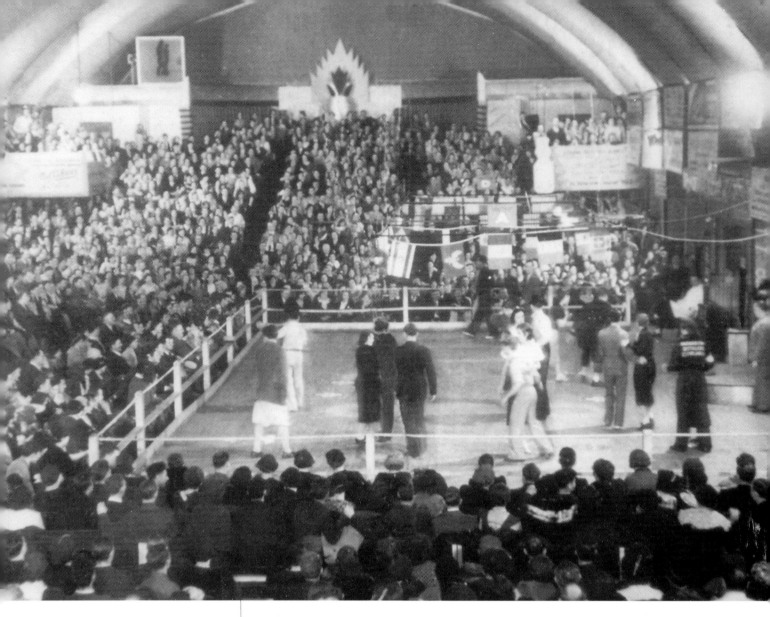

The Race of Nations Walkathon was held in the park's ballroom in 1934.
EDWARD C. LEARNER COLLECTION

Guarding the midway in winter.
EDWARD C. LEARNER COLLECTION

in the park's ballroom. Each contestant was identified by ethnic background, and the flags of all nations represented were displayed. International marathon rules were used, and floor judges eliminated anyone not able to keep moving. During the marathon the couples took turns singing and dancing, and WKBN broadcast the contest three times a day. One couple got married during the contest and said they would use the walkathon as their honeymoon. A 480-pound cake was served to the guests. After four weeks thirteen couples remained in the contest, and by mutual consent the rules were modified. The prize money was pooled and $24 set aside each day. R. M. Edwards of New York, who managed the contest, explained how the money was distributed under the new rules. "Each contestant, upon dropping out, received his or her share of the $24 a day due from the time the agreements were signed until these contestants dropped out. A total of $1,320 was divided among the contestants in this manner for 24 days the contest operated. Twenty-six contestants shared in the money after the agreements were made."

"Something Doing Every Minute" was the new slogan for Idora's 1935 season. The parking fee was set at 20 cents, but the motorists received four 5-cent ride tickets. The free midway acts included Routon's educated alley dogs and donkey baseball games. Idora's baseball fans saw high quality games as well; the St. Stanislaus amateur world champion baseball team picked Idora as its home field and played many games there. The latest addition to Idora's rides was the Dragon. In the dance pavilion Eddie Conti's Orchestra opened followed by the orchestras of Tommy Christian, George Duffy, and Gene Beecher.

Picnic bookings were greatly improved for the 1935 season. The schedule listed over fifty picnic bookings with companies such as General Fireproofing, Republic Rubber, Youngstown Sheet and Tube, and Westinghouse Electric bringing their employees to the park for a day of fun. Church groups, schools, lodges, and more than a dozen ethnic groups also booked picnic days. The installation of permanent floodlights at the ball field enabled picnickers and teams to use the diamond at night.

Occasionally, misinformation about Idora's history has been published, and the park itself, intentionally or unintentionally, sometimes caused the confusion. Manager Charles Deibel announced that August 19-23, 1935, would be given over to a celebration of the park's fortieth anniversary, and the *Vindicator* reported that "Idora's site was brought [sic] from Bales M. Campbell and the park was built in 1895." Neither fact was correct. Bales Campbell, a prominent Youngstown attorney who served on the Board of City Commissioners, was instrumental in developing real estate parcels on the city's south side, but he never owned the Idora property. Idora began in 1899, not 1895, so 1935 was the park's thirty-sixth anniversary (or, stated another way, the park's thirty-seventh summer). The mistake in the park's founding date would be perpetuated for the next forty years.

In any event, the park had a great celebration. Manager Deibel announced a 50 percent price reduction on rides from 1:30 p.m. to midnight all week, and several special sporting events were scheduled. On Monday and Tuesday the Ohio state softball championship was played in the ballpark. A wrestling match was held on Wednesday, and the Golden Gloves amateur boxing tournament on

Trolley loading station located near the ballroom.
RICK SHALE COLLECTION

The ballroom anchored the lower midway.
MARCELLA DUFFY COLLECTION

1931 - 1945

Water was pumped from the Rapids channel to the Old Mill to create a waterfall.
MARCELLA DUFFY COLLECTION

Thursday.

Because of heavy picnic bookings, Idora opened two weeks earlier than normal in 1936. Business conditions had improved enough that the park owners were able to spend $40,000 on improvements.

A kiddie coaster designed by Ed Vettel, who worked for the Harton-owned West View Park in Pittsburgh, was built in 1936 and placed at the north end of the park where other kiddie rides were located. (It would later be moved to the northeast corner of the park and eventually to its final location adjacent to Kiddieland.)

Landscaping had suffered during the early years of the Depression, but in 1936 hundreds of fir trees were planted, as were a thousand giant petunia plants. The old bandstand was converted into an aviary housing tropical birds, and fifty-six monkeys took up annual summer residence on Monkey Island. The wooden seats in the ballpark were replaced with steel and concrete bleachers. A new ride called the Loop-O-Plane manufactured by Eyerly Aircraft of Salem, Oregon, was installed, and new scenic effects were added to the Old Mill. Multi-colored glass was installed in the windmill arms, and spotlights flashed on the glass at night to create a dazzling effect.

By the mid-1930s Idora ended its long tradition of presenting live theater and vaudeville. After standing vacant for a few seasons, the theater was torn down and replaced by new midway games and refreshment stands.

Those who arrived at Idora by streetcar in 1937 found the trolley stop relocated. The street cars still came down Parkview Avenue but now made the turn on the site of the old parking lot in the northeast corner of the park where new loading and unloading shelters were constructed. Those coming by automobile found the parking lot expanded and coated with heavy oil to combat the annual problem of flying dust.

Several new attractions were introduced. A miniature train with six brightly painted cars now carried passengers along the old trolley route on the western boundary of the park. Mounted on a forty-foot pylon, the Stratoship combined the sensation of an airplane and a balloon ride, and the newspaper called it "more thrilling but less upsetting than last year's Loop-O-Plane." This new ride was manufactured in nearby Beaver Falls, Pennsylvania, by the R. E. Chambers Company, which had succeeded Traver Engineering. New to the midway were

"Shok Shu," a ghostly hall of terrors with Chinese torture chambers, and "Raisynell," a dark ride.

Because of heavy picnic bookings and spring parties, Idora in 1938 again opened in mid-May, two weeks earlier than the usual date. The first week was marked by a fireworks show and free acts on the midway, which included the Wolandi Duo performing acrobatics and Doris McKenzie playing organ concerts. Sammy Kaye and his Orchestra entertained in the dance pavilion for the first two weeks of the season. Among the out-of-town companies planning picnics at Idora were the Hoover Sweeper Company of Canton, the General Dry Battery Company of Cleveland, and several companies from western Pennsylvania. Manager Deibel estimated that the picnics would bring more than 200,000 visitors from northeastern Ohio and western Pennsylvania.

For most of the 1930s the park employed about 150 summer employees. By 1938 visitors knew what to expect from Charlie Deibel when the park opened: fresh paint, fresh sand on Idora Beach, free acts on the midway, fireworks, and a name band headlining in the dance pavilion. The picnics grew more and more popular, and Idora continued to provide free gas grills and hot plates for guests to prepare meals and hot beverages.

The owners continued to spend money in the off season to improve the park and provide new attractions. Two baboons and several baby monkeys joined the colony on Monkey Island. Some of the changes were actually old attractions making a return to the park. For example, a bowling alley on the midway was added, and the Fun House was remodeled in 1938. New rides included the Humpty Dump, which carried passengers in small cars on an up-and-down ride in the dark, and the Flying Octopus, which the park acquired from the Great Lakes Exposition in Cleveland.

The Octopus, built by the Eyerly Aircraft Corporation of Salem, Oregon, was an eight-car ride, each car accommodating two large adults, three medium-built adults, or three or four children, making an average capacity of twenty adults or thirty children. The Flying Octopus was

Interior of the Heidelberg.
EDWARD C. LEARNER COLLECTION

Relaxing on the midway.
MARTHA NEAG COLLECTION PROVIDED BY EDWARD C. LEARNER

Idora developed a new fun house in the 1930s.
COURTESY OF HISTORIC IMAGES

1931 - 1945

The old fun house was converted into a roller skating rink.
EDWARD C. LEARNER COLLECTION

In the fall roller skating moved to the ballroom.
RICK SHALE COLLECTION

one of the first rides covered with lights, having 144 light sockets on the sweeps. It cost the park twice as much— $6,550—but had a much higher ride capacity than the Loop-O-Plane, which also had been built by Eyerly.

To help inaugurate the new season, Uncle Bill, an NBC radio talent scout, held a talent contest in the ballpark. He brought with him several past winners including an acrobat, a six-year-old accordionist, a fourteen-year-old tap dance champion, and the "Pint Size Hillbillies," who played ukuleles and harmonicas.

Dick Stabile, a saxophone artist from Pittsburgh's Hotel William Penn, opened the season in the ballroom and was followed by Herbie Holmes and his Orchestra. Ruth Autenreith's Orchestra was engaged for Heidelberg Gardens.

The *Vindicator* sponsored its fifteenth Kiddies' Day, and fifteen thousand jammed the park for a day of athletic contests, penny scrambles, free dancing, and three-cent ride tickets.

Idora found itself "snakebitten" by rumor at the end of the 1938 season. Everyone seemed to be asking "did you hear the story of the girl who was bitten by a poisonous snake in one of the park 'rolly-coaster' cars and died before the car could stop?" The tale could not be substantiated with anything resembling proof, but the rumor refused to die. According to the *Vindicator*, "The story is that one girl–or maybe it was two or three girls–was bitten by a rattlesnake–or maybe it was a copperhead or a runaway boa constrictor–in the Wildcat–or maybe it was the Jack Rabbit or the Old Mill–at Idora Park–or maybe it was some other park." The Idora management and the newspaper attempted to trace the rumor but could find no basis for the allegations. A second rumor claimed that the Idora owners had paid the *Vindicator* $50,000 to suppress the story. The *Vindicator* editorialized against such rumormongering, and Charlie Deibel offered $500 to anyone who could prove either that someone had died of snakebite at Idora or that the park had bribed the newspaper to kill the story.

Through the years public interest in roller skating rose and fell; Idora followed these trends and generally offered skating when its popularity was on the rise. At the end of the 1938 summer dancing season, Idora converted the dance pavilion to the Idora Park Roller Skating Palace. A special maple floor was laid over the dance floor and a thousand pairs of skates were purchased. Skating was held nightly from 8 p.m. to 11 p.m. It cost 35 cents to skate or 10 cents to watch. The roller skating proved so popular that in 1939 a new outdoor rink was constructed adjacent to Idora's north entrance off Parkview Avenue. The terrazzo floor measured 70 by 160 feet.

The swimming pool opened under new ownership in 1939. After fifteen years, the Idora Natatorium Company chose not to renew its lease on the pool, and the Idora Amusement Company acquired the attraction for an undisclosed sum. Of more interest to the bathers was the conversion to salt water bathing. Manager Deibel explained that engineers drilled to a depth of 650 feet and tapped into a natural flow of salt water sufficient to fill the pool daily. Pool prices were reduced to 25 cents for adults with season passes listed at $6.00. Children swam for a dime in the morning or 15 cents in the afternoon and paid $4.00 for a season pass. Free swimming lessons were available to season ticket holders.

Tiny Hill and his Orchestra kicked off the dance season, and to attract more dancers a portion of the dance floor was set aside for "jitterbugs" enabling them to swing without disturbing the traditional dancers. Park plan dance prices (where one paid by the dance) were reduced to 5 cents a dance or six tickets for a quarter. Mondays were designated as bargain nights with social plan dancing all night for 25 cents. Heidelberg Gardens opened under new management with a no cover, no minimum policy.

For the 16th annual *Vindicator* Kiddies' Day held June 21, 1939, the first fifty children to arrive received free ride tickets. Some enterprising youngsters showed up at 1 a.m. to stake their claim, and when they found they could not spend the night in a park shelter house, they hiked up the street to find a place to sleep. The *Vindicator* reported that every hour or so, two of the group would return to the park to make sure their places were secure. By five a.m. 175 kids were at the gates waiting for the 8 a.m. opening! Contests for swimming, diving, pie eating, and watermelon eating were staged. Ride prices were reduced to three cents, and free dancing was provided in the afternoon.

More than twelve thousand area high school students opened the season on the eighth annual High School Day, sponsored by the *Vindicator*, Mahoning Valley Hi-Y Clubs, and Idora. Visitors to the midway could try Cinderella's Slipper, a dark ride where passengers rode in huge slippers. Kiddyland featured the kiddie coaster, the Gondola Glide, and a dwarf aeroplane swing.

The *Vindicator* published a nostalgic editorial on May 13, 1939, to celebrate the park's fortieth anniversary (which the park erroneously had celebrated four years earlier):

Idora Park, opening for its 40th season [actually the 41st], provides an example of stout resistance to modern encroachments on old-time amusements. The theater languishes and even the circus totters. There is heavy mortality among the parks, too, but Idora and a few other stout old enterprises go merrily on in spite of the radio and the automobile and the movies. . . .

There is still dancing, but by jitterbugs instead of waltzers. Replacing a "steady" orchestra which played a Sunday concert because people didn't dance on the Sabbath, there is a new "name" band every week or two. . . .

Public address systems have come to add to the general air of gayety, broadcast the whereabouts of lost children, and distract the park's

An eagle, purchased from the Great Lakes Exposition in Cleveland, adorned the Parkview entrance.
COURTESY OF HISTORIC IMAGES

The annual Youth On Parade pageant featured decorated buggies and bicycles.
MARGARET KOZAR COLLECTION
PROVIDED BY EDWARD C. LEARNER

1931 - 1945

Walking on the upper midway, 1940.
COURTESY OF HISTORIC IMAGES

Youngstown Sheet and Tube Company Labor Day picnic, 1938.
OHIO HISTORICAL SOCIETY

neighbors. One hopes that a merciful management will soften the loud speaker's raucous voice this season.

But much remains unchanged. The merry-go-round (was there ever a happier, apter name?) still goes round and round; popcorn and pop may be had; the girls still shriek as the roller coaster swoops—and there still are provisions for the old time picnic.

The editorial concluded by emphasizing the connection between picnics and the financial health of the nation's remaining parks.

Idora continued to attract a lot of large industrial picnics. The number of employees and their families attending some of these picnics sometimes even exceeded the holiday crowds. For example, the 1939 Youngstown Sheet and Tube Company picnic drew a crowd of more than twenty thousand. The day's activities included a flag-raising ceremony with music by the Sheet and Tube band, a concert by the Sheet and Tube male chorus, employee baseball games, and free dancing in the pavilion with music provided by the Sheet and Tube Orchestra. Typical activities for the company picnics were penny scrambles for the kids, prize giveaways for the adults, and contests such as wheelbarrow races, egg and spoon races, ring and toothpick races, three-legged races, egg tosses, and slipper-kicking races. Eating, dancing, and enjoying the rides completed the schedule.

Minor league baseball returned to Idora in 1939 when Youngstown again acquired a franchise in the Middle Atlantic League, called by baseball historian Robert Obojski "the toughest Class C circuit in the history of organized baseball." The Youngstown Browns were affiliated with the St. Louis Browns (later the Baltimore Orioles) who visited Idora for an exhibition game.

The 1940 season brought more changes to Idora. The Wildcat underwent a re-profiling. The original first drop was an aeroplane dip or curve that began the descent while the cars were still in the curve. With the rebuilt hill, coaster cars coming off the chainlift traveled completely around the first curve before beginning the descent. The new first drop proved to be just as exciting as the original hill, and it required less maintenance. The park announced a contest to rename the remodeled coaster, but nothing came of the idea and the coaster remained the Wildcat until the park closed.

A new Whip and the Rumpus Bumpus, a dark ride from National Amusement Device Company, Dayton, Ohio, were added. Bud Hawkins and his Animal Circus entertained on the midway. Monday night was again designated bargain night in the dance pavilion with dancing all night for 25 cents. Thursday was Surprise Night with a 35-cent admission. Carl Lorch and his Orchestra opened the season and played for a week before moving on to Euclid Beach Park in Cleveland. Orchestras often moved from park to park in eastern Ohio and western Pennsylvania.

Charlie Deibel turned seventy-three years old on September 1, 1940, but showed no signs of slowing down after nine years as park manager and sixteen years as principal owner. "I'm the only man who made this park pay," said Deibel. "I'm rather pleased about that. I like being on the job here, meeting the

The Youngstown Browns on the Idora ball field.
© THE VINDICATOR, 1999

people, old and new friends alike." Deibel had reason to be proud. Picnic bookings were ahead of schedule, and a near-record crowd of fifteen thousand showed up for the ninth annual High School Day.

The impact of the war in Europe was already being felt on the home front in 1941–even at Idora. In its report on the season opener, the *Vindicator* wrote, "Keeping in step with the trend in this bomb-pitted world, the park management has added an exciting new ride 'The Blackout' to the many favorites of children and adults in the valley." The Blackout dark ride would be re-themed, remodeled, and renamed several times over the next forty years. Also added were a new Ferris wheel and a Tumble Bug. The latter was built by the R. E. Chambers Company, from nearby Beaver Falls, Pennsylvania. The purchase of these two rides was fortuitously timed since no rides would be manufactured during the war. Kiddyland, though not on the scale of the children's area that would emerge in the 1950s, was a safe, fenced-in park-within-the-park. (The park used various names and spellings for its children's area. For example, "Kiddy Park" was used for much of the 1950s. For clarity the "Kiddyland" spelling is used when referring to the children's area of the 1930s and 1940s; "Kiddieland" is used for the area that replaced the swimming pool in 1951.)

Dancing, which had really come into its own in the 1930s, remained popular during the war years–1941 to 1945–and Heidelberg Gardens offered dancing as well as food every night except Monday. The ballroom continued to offer social plan dancing (dancing all evening for one price) on Mondays and Thursdays, and park plan dancing (a nickel a dance) on other nights. George Hall and his Hotel Taft Orchestra opened the 1941 season. Hall's band featured Dolly Dawn and the Dawn Patrol, a band-within-the-band.

The Youngstown Browns played their third and final season at Idora in 1941 and then disbanded as did the Ak-

By the 1940s more people came to Idora by car than by trolley.
MARCELLA DUFFY COLLECTION

1931 - 1945

In 1939 Idora opened a new outdoor roller skating rink located in the northeast corner of the park. When the summer season ended, skating moved to the ballroom.
ALL PHOTOS FROM THE EDWARD C. LEARNER COLLECTION

ron club, leaving the Middle Atlantic League with only six teams in 1942. World War II took so many players that after the 1942 season the entire league suspended operations, and minor league play did not resume until 1946. But the Youngstown Browns were not the only professional baseball players at Idora in 1941. In July the Negro National League staged a contest at the park. The Homestead Grays returned to Idora for the first time in three years and beat the Philadelphia Stars 8-3.

Although the United States did not enter the war until December 1941, the conflict in Europe was felt by many of Idora's visitors that summer. In August the Clan MacDonald, a Scottish group, held an outing at Idora. Their theme was V for Victory, and money collected went to British War Relief.

World War II had an impact on the amusement park business in many ways. Idora prospered financially during the war but had a hard time finding and keeping employees. Attendance at the annual High School Day dropped in 1942 to eight thousand, but the picnic bookings were steady, and Assistant Manager Max Rindin predicted a profitable season for Idora, which was, *Billboard* noted, "located in the heart of the steel industry with its peak operations and record payrolls." Resort parks like Cedar Point, which drew customers from greater distances, were hit hard during the war because of restrictions placed on train travel and the rationing of gasoline, tires, and passenger cars.

The war also required some name changes. With anti-German sentiment running high, the park management switched the name of Heidelberg Gardens to the less inflammatory Idora Gardens. The name would not revert to Heidelberg Gardens until 1949. Patrons were now urged to "Relax and Refresh at Idora Gardens."

On August 30th Idora held a Send-Off Day for all the inductees and enlistees in the area. The Send-Off Committee,

In the 1930s and 1940s nearly every prominent big band orchestra played in Idora's ballroom.
CHARLES J. JACQUES, JR. COLLECTION

Maintenance workers clowning on the midway.
MARGARET KOZAR COLLECTION
PROVIDED BY EDWARD C. LEARNER

In 1940 Charlie Deibel, Max Rindin, and Pat Duffy, Sr. scouted the New York World's Fair for ideas.
MARCELLA DUFFY COLLECTION

1931 - 1945

The upper midway in the 1940s.
MARCELLA DUFFY COLLECTION

Park employees with young Pat Duffy, Jr. in the foreground.
MARGARET KOZAR COLLECTION
PROVIDED BY EDWARD C. LEARNER

representing forty-eight organizations, gave sewing kits, cigarettes, and other gifts to the departing soldiers. The cigarettes were collected in "Give A Pack" kegs that were set up throughout the park. A baseball game between American Legion teams was held, and the Youngstown Military Band provided concerts throughout the day.

Idora also held a Tin Can Party to help the Tin Salvage Committee in Youngstown. Youngsters could exchange the cans for ride tickets. All rides "cost" three tin cans for kids and six cans for adults. Six thousand children participated and deposited an estimated 175,000 cans weighing approximately twenty tons.

The Youngstown Sheet and Tube Company held its annual Field Day picnic at Idora on Labor Day, noting that some men would have to work that day "producing for war," but their families could still have a good time. A bathing beauty contest drew a lot of interest. On the midway was displayed a huge working model Hot Strip Mill. Certain activities were segregated, and the company's African American employees were permitted to use the dance hall for only one hour from noon to 1 p.m.

In 1943 the park added a Magic Carpet stunt to the Fun House, and "Laughing Sal," whose raucous laughter never ceased, made her debut. The Magic Carpet was located near the exit of the Fun House. A patron or couple would sit on a bench, which tipped them onto a canvas sheet moving over rollers. When riders reached the last roller, they were dumped off. The Carpet and mechanical laughing lady were both manufactured by the Philadelphia Toboggan Company.

During the war some midway games were given a topical theme. Patrons were urged to demonstrate their pitching skill to "Slap a Jap" and "Tip a Tank." Servicemen from nearby Camp Reynolds (near Greenville, Pennsylvania) would visit Idora before shipping out to Europe. Many of Idora's wartime ads stressed good health: "Keep Fit! Relax . . . Have Fun and Work. Buy Bonds For Victory." Idora's swimming pool advertised "Keep Fit! Salt Water is healthful."

The management eliminated park plan dancing where one paid by the dance and went with a social plan dance policy exclusively. Mondays remained bargain night at 30 cents; Saturdays and Sundays were 50 cents, and all other nights were 40 cents. High School Day was sponsored, as usual, by the *Vindicator* and the Mahoning County Hi-Y Clubs. The newspaper predicted a good crowd, "even though priorities and other war-time necessity prohibit the usual list of prizes and rides at reduced cost."

In 1944 the park added two new attractions: the Aerial Joy Ride and the Honeymoon Trail. The Aerial Joy Ride was similar to the old circle swing and had been a hit at the New York World's Fair of 1939-40. A tall mast surrounded by four pylons supported a ring from which hung small airplanes. The riders would fly through the air at a high speed. The Honeymoon Trail was a walk-

The Rapids boats featured a dragon figurehead.
EDWARD C. LEARNER COLLECTION

Many GI's visited the park during World War II.
MARTHA NEAG COLLECTION PROVIDED BY EDWARD C. LEARNER

Wartime game booth.
EDWARD C. LEARNER COLLECTION

1931 - 1945

Posing on the Octopus.
MARGARET KOZAR COLLECTION
PROVIDED BY EDWARD C. LEARNER

Idora Park employees traveled to West View Park in Pittsburgh for an annual picnic.
COURTESY OF MIKE TARANTINO
IDORA PARK DEVELOPMENT COMPANY

through attraction housed in a building at the south end of the park near where the Turtle was later installed. Couples stepped on pads that would trip switches to light up scenes in the darkened passages.

With the 1944 season not yet a month old, tragedy struck Idora. On May 28th 13-year-old James Rogers drowned in the Idora swimming pool. Three weeks later on June 16th two more drownings occurred. Dead were two sisters, Gloria and Dolores DeAngelis, age 13 and 12. The pool had been crowded with people trying to cope with 92-degree heat. When the girls did not return home Friday night, their parents called the police. The bodies were found the following day, and police theorized that one girl had gone under and the other had died trying to save her sister. The coroner ruled the deaths accidental drowning and revealed that neither girl could swim.

The *Vindicator* published an editorial on the drownings, pointing out that city-operated pools had not experienced a drowning in twelve years. The last death in a city pool, said the newspaper, "was the case of a woman who had a heart attack and drowned in a foot of water." The paper was critical of the Idora pool's circular design. "In a circular pool, shallow at the perimeter and deepening to the middle, it is less easy for the bather to know at all times just where he is or where he is going in relation to water depth." The paper added that Idora's deep water was marked by a series of unconnected buoys at the five-foot depth.

As a result of the deaths, several changes were made. The diving tower was removed, and the pool bottom was painted white to eliminate shadows. A concrete terrace replaced the sand beach that had formerly surrounded the pool. A fenced-in wading pool was set up in front of the lifeguard stand, and a continuous cable was installed marking the four-foot depth.

The U. S. Army staged a small "war" at Idora in September. A cast of 350 servicemen presented "Steel Delivers the Punch," a tribute to the valley's steel production sponsored by the War Department and Youngstown's War Manpower Commission. Weapons were demonstrated, and several war heroes were introduced. The finale was an attack on a "Jap pillbox." "With armored-truck fire spraying the area," reported the *Vindicator*, "the infantry, armed with pistols, rifles, machine guns and Browning automatic rifles, poured bullets into the pillbox. Anti-aircraft guns boomed in the rear. Many were 'wounded' and medical corpsmen crawled between them giving first aid. Then two flame-throwers were worked close to the pillbox. A blast from

A large American flag adorned the bathhouse during the war.
MARTHA NEAG COLLECTION PROVIDED BY EDWARD C. LEARNER

Idora's pool remained popular in the early 1940s.
RICK SHALE COLLECTION

them turned it into a big mess. The targets reached, a Jap flag was ripped from its pole and the American flag raised. The band played 'The Star-Spangled Banner' to end the 'war.'"

With the exception of the safety measures in the pool, the park made few changes for the 1945 season. The buildings sported a fresh coat of paint, but the shortages of wartime materials and help were noticeable. Live ammunition for the shooting gallery and even hot dogs remained in short supply. Lumber was often substituted for metal, and the park's maintenance staff became quite creative at making do despite these shortages.

In mid-August World War II ended, and the government immediately canceled gasoline rationing, though sugar, meat, and rubber tires and footwear continued to be rationed. The nation celebrated victory and eagerly anticipated a return to peacetime conditions. Although Idora had suffered fewer hardships during the war than most parks, many activities had been put on hold for the duration. Now the park owners could begin to plan for much-needed repairs and new attractions to accommodate patrons in the post-war era.

1946-1954

6 THE POST-WAR PERIOD

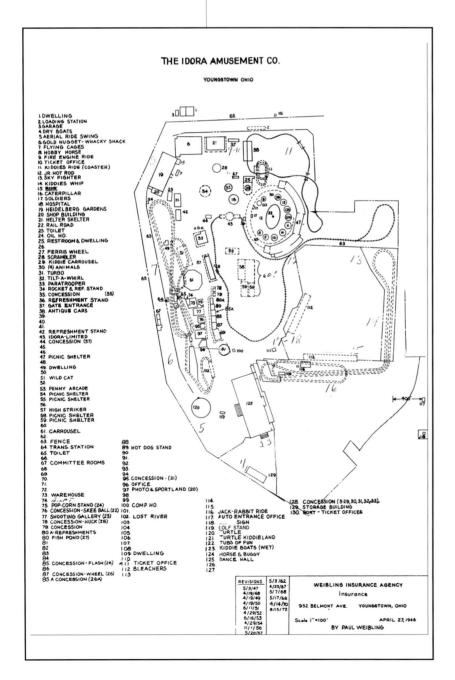

Once the war was over, the mills and factories of the Mahoning Valley cut back to peacetime production schedules, but Idora's high level of activity continued. With the end of wartime rationing, passenger cars, tires, and gasoline became available again, and to better accommodate the growing number of visitors who came to Idora by car, the parking lot was paved with asphalt. Returning military personnel provided more visitors and also eased the park's shortage of employees. Families came in record numbers, and Charlie Deibel reported that Idora had its most successful year ever in 1946.

It took a while for the ride manufacturers to return to civilian production and even longer for them to develop new, innovative attractions. Despite the difficulty in acquiring new rides, Idora was able to add the Auto Skooter bumper cars in 1946, and to reintroduce an old favorite, the pony track.

Postwar prices for the dance pavilion climbed to 75 cents for Sundays and holidays, and 60 cents for other nights. Cecil Golly and his "Music By Golly" opened the season. The management reminded visitors that no beer or intoxicating liquor would be sold in the ballroom, a policy appropriate for a location used for so many school functions.

Fire safety became an issue at Idora Park in the spring of 1946. Youngstown Fire Chief Clarence Thomas visited the park in May and ordered Heidelberg Gardens and the Fun House closed, condemning them as fire hazards. A blaze at Youngstown's Hotel Pick-Ohio a week earlier had prompted the chief to initiate a vigorous campaign for fire safety in public buildings. Park officials acted immediately on the Fire Chief's suggestions. A new doorway was cut in Heidelberg Gardens and fire extinguishers were installed. Additional exits were also created for the Fun House. A day later the Fire Chief re-inspected and declared the buildings safe. Neither building had to be closed. (The newspaper referred to the park's restaurant as Heidelberg Gardens, the name most patrons knew, but the park continued to use the name Idora Gardens in its newspaper ads.)

Minor league baseball returned to Idora in 1946. The Middle Atlantic League resumed operation, and Youngstown rejoined the Class C loop. The local franchise was known as the Youngstown Gremlins after the mischievous invisible creatures that plagued World War II flyers. Joining Youngstown in the reorganized league were Erie, Johnstown, Butler, Oil City, and Niagara Falls.

In 1947 Charlie Deibel celebrated his twenty-third season as part owner of Idora, but several employees could claim even greater longevity. Pat Duffy, Sr., manager of concessions and games, had been at Idora since 1905. Sam Boncilla, the ground maintenance man, had begun his Idora career as a day laborer in 1910. The Hoover family had run the photo gallery for almost forty years, and Nellie James had been the cashier at the ballroom for thirty-seven years. Robert Mills, foreman of rides, had a quarter century of service, and Joe Croslin, in charge of the Wildcat and Jack Rabbit, had become a nationally recognized coaster expert during his thirty-five years at Idora. Many others had worked at Idora for more than two decades.

Baseball and boxing continued to attract crowds to Idora. After one season as the Gremlins, Youngstown's Middle Atlantic League team changed its name to the Colts for the 1947 season. The Negro Leagues continued to make regular stops at Idora, and in August the Cleveland Buckeyes of the Negro American League played the Asheville Blues, defending champs of the Negro Southern League.

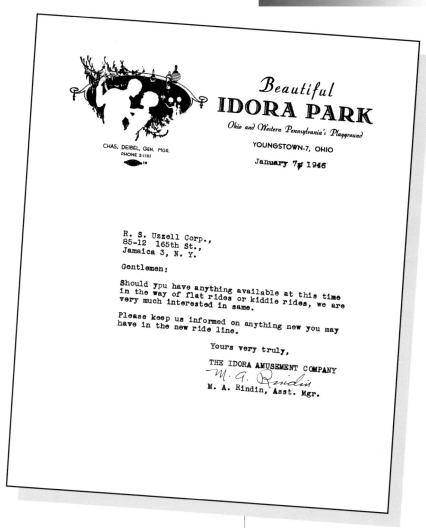

Rocky Graziano, the reigning middleweight champion, boxed a four-round exhibition at the Idora ball field. For visitors who preferred to participate rather than watch sports, Idora offered outdoor roller skating every night from 8 to 11 p.m.

The Great Monkey Escape occurred during the summer of 1947, and it quickly became one of Idora's biggest publicity stories. On August 24th over two dozen monkeys bolted from their cage near the north entrance to the park. Groundskeeper Sam Boncilla speculated that the simians had taken a badly needed vacation. "If you had to put up with a lot of strange faces peering at you inside a cage all day long, you'd need a vacation too," he said. In any case the escape was a publicity bonanza.

For days the *Vindicator* reported various sightings. Ten monkeys returned

Charlie Deibel, manager in the 1930s and part owner.
MARTHA NEAG COLLECTION PROVIDED BY EDWARD C. LEARNER

1946 - 1954

Nationality Days often featured traditional costumes.
MIKE RONCONE COLLECTION

Youngstown's minor league baseball team was called the Gremlins in 1946.
EDWARD C. LEARNER COLLECTION

to the park but preferred to sit on the roof of the Fun House rather than get back in their cage. By mid-October many of the monkeys were still at large. Five had been recaptured and sent to a zoo in Canton for the winter, and seven or eight of the more vicious monkeys had been destroyed as a safety measure. Half a dozen had just disappeared, and the remaining half dozen or so were assumed to spend the winter in Mill Creek Park. Manager Max Rindin reported that those still at large had been kept well fed by residents in the Mill Creek area.

Such monkey escapes seem to have happened at many amusement parks in the 1930s and 1940s. Even the *New York Times* reported an escape from Coney Island's Luna Park. Monkeys also escaped from Kennywood, Meyers Lake, and Waldameer.

New rides for the 1948 season included a Caterpillar and the Rocket Ships. The Circle Swing had anchored the upper midway for years. The original wicker gondolas had been replaced by a larger swing with open-cockpit propeller planes. These planes were now replaced by shiny silver rocket ships from R. E. Chambers, which gave the ride a futuristic look that appealed to the Buck Rogers generation.

The Caterpillar was a new model of the thrill ride that initially had been introduced at Idora in the 1920s. Also new was a Baby Boat Ride for the children. Six red, white, and blue gasoline-powered boats, each holding five youngsters, automatically followed a circular course in two feet of water. The ride was set up in the south end of the park near the pony track.

The Youngstown Colts again played their Middle Atlantic League games at Idora, to the dismay of some of the park's neighbors who complained about late games running past midnight. Fifth Ward councilman Harry Jacobs asked league officials if games could be called when the park closed.

In August the Wildcat was the scene of another death. Royal Dinkleman of Salem was thrown from the coaster and died of a fractured skull. The twenty-year old and his companions had ridden the coaster several times before the accident. Witnesses said that Dinkleman had put his feet over the safety lap bar and had apparently stood up as the coaster traveled over the second hill. The coroner ruled the death an accident.

In January 1949 Idora experienced a change in ownership, and control passed to Max Rindin, L. A. "Tony" Cavalier, Jr., and Pat Duffy, Sr. The new owners acquired stock formerly held by Thomas Murray, Jr. Charles Deibel and his son Victor retained their shares. Duffy was elected president of the company, and Victor Deibel vice-president. Max Rindin became secretary and Tony Cavalier treasurer. Eighty-one-year-old Charlie Deibel was named Chairman of the Board.

The new owners had plenty of experience on which to draw. Pat Duffy, Sr. had been involved with concessions at the park since 1905. Max Rindin had started at Idora in 1925 as an assistant to Charlie Deibel. After serving as assistant manager for several seasons, he had become manager in 1941, a position he retained after becoming part owner. Although Tony Cavalier had less experience at Idora, he was no stranger to promoting entertainment. As owner of the Elms Ballroom since 1932, he had promoted virtually all of the major orchestras of the big band era. From 1936 to 1944 he owned and

The Jack Rabbit provided a backdrop for Idora's ball field.
EDWARD C. LEARNER COLLECTION

operated The Mansion, a popular nightspot for dining and dancing. He had promoted some dances at Idora and also had experience as a building contractor.

The first major change that the new owners made was to close the swimming pool, which had opened in 1924. In its place was created Motor Boat Lagoon. Gasoline-powered, two-seater motorboats would now cruise the waters formerly used by the swimmers. No reason was given for the conversion, but evidence strongly suggests the move was made to defuse racial tensions stemming from integrated swimming. Two suits charging racial discrimination had been filed against the Idora Roller Skating Rink in early April, and the owners may have seen the pool as a potential source of trouble. Shrinking revenue was another factor. By 1949 the city of Youngstown operated half a dozen municipal swimming pools, so Idora's was hardly a unique attraction. The city had opened the new John Chase pool in 1948 and charged a lower admission than Idora.

The owners constructed a new building at the north end of the park to house the Auto Skooters and ordered new cars manufactured by Lusse in Philadelphia, Pennsylvania. These bumper cars ran on a steel floor, used a higher voltage, and threw more sparks than the old Dodgem cars, which they replaced.

In addition to the Auto Skooters and Motor Boat Lagoon, the park offered in 1949 the Wildcat, Jack Rabbit, Merry-Go-Round, Caterpillar, Whip, Rapids, Rocket Ships, Ferris Wheel, Blackout, Barrel of Fun, Penny Arcade, Shooting Gallery, and Pony Track. Several other attractions including the junior coaster were designated for the kids. The name of the park restaurant was changed from Idora Gardens back to the more familiar Heidelberg Gardens.

Russ Romero and his Orchestra opened the 1949 dancing season, which offered special features seven nights a week. Monday remained Bargain Night, and Tuesday was Organization Night with the ballroom available to any religious, civic, or fraternal group wishing to have exclusive use. Wednesday was Over-30 Night when Pappy Howard's Orchestra would play the old favorites such as the waltz, Cuban waltz, schottische, heel and toe, and Virginia reel. Thursday was designated Novelty Night, and Friday was Polka Night. The biggest crowds were expected on the weekends. Arthur Murray's dance instructors were on hand Saturdays to teach beginners. Some of the bands booked for Idora in 1949 included Guy Lombardo, Vaughn Monroe, Charlie Barnet, and Nick Bari.

Organization Night apparently at-

Basketball toss game in the late 1940s.
LARRY/JIM KENNEDY COLLECTION
PROVIDED BY EDWARD C. LEARNER

1946 - 1954

Idora's swimming pool closed after the 1948 season.
MARCELLA DUFFY COLLECTION

tracted few bookings; by mid-summer the park announced that the Youngstown Symphony Orchestra under conductor Michael Ficocelli would play a pops concert every Tuesday night.

The season got under way with an Easter weekend preview. Visitors to this "spring" opening were greeted by snow and swirling winds, but the weather did not seem to deter the crowd from riding the coasters and having fun. Park officials played "Winter Wonderland" over the public address system.

When Guy Lombardo played on May 26th, 1,700 loyal fans showed up for "the sweetest music this side of heaven," and the *Vindicator* called the event "the greatest dance revival here in years." The old-timers far outnumbered the jitterbugs. The *Vindicator* reported, "There were hundreds in the 'social security' bracket–gray haired and without a spring in their step–who never stopped dancing. . . . The call of Lombardo brought them out of the armchairs–in furs, in strapless evening gowns, in tai- lored suits. The dress was as varied as the crowd."

Mid-Atlantic League baseball continued to be played in Idora's ball park, and in 1949 the Youngstown team changed its name for the third time in four years. The Colts became the Youngstown Athletics when the major league Philadelphia Athletics moved its Class C farm club to town.

At the end of each season the park's monkeys were shipped to the Canton Zoo for the winter, but in 1949 the owners offered the monkeys for sale at $25 each and were deluged with offers. A new troop of monkeys was ordered for next season.

A new Tilt-a-Whirl, purchased from Sellner Manufacturing Company, was added to Idora's rides in 1950, and Motor Boat Lagoon operated for a second and final year. Monday night dancing was eliminated, and Polka Night was expanded to Tuesdays and Thursdays. Friday was designated Teen-Age Night. Though rock and roll was still a few years away, the Friday teen nights were the early ancestor of the popular record hops of the mid-1950s and 1960s.

In mid-July the French fries stand caught on fire and was destroyed. The blaze occurred after the park had closed for the day, and firefighters were able to contain the fire before it spread to the nearby Rocket Ship ride. Ethel and Bob Wood operated the stand, and the French fries they made were one of the park's most popular foods.

In the fall the water was drained from Motor Boat Lagoon, and the old swimming pool was filled in, a task that required more than 6,700 cubic yards of dirt. This project marked the first step in the most extensive renovation in Idora's history.

Following World War II, returning servicemen had shifted their focus from fighting to families, and America experienced a baby boom. As these children grew old enough to walk and enjoy visits to the park, the traditional amusement parks responded by developing or expanding special children's areas within their grounds. By spring of 1951 Idora's Kiddieland had risen on the site of the old pool. The distinctive semi-circular amphitheater was retained with the former bathhouse converted to picnic facilities seating a thousand. The new Kiddieland, or Idora Kiddy Park as it was often called in the 1950s, contained thirteen rides and was designed for children one to eight. Among the new attractions were a miniature Ferris wheel, hobby horse, sky fighter, and hook and ladder ride. The park also bought for the children a new scale model

Crosley fire truck, and Manager Max Rindin drove Youngstown Mayor Charles P. Henderson and Fire Chief Leroy Halstead on the first ride.

The twenty-first annual Hi-Y-Tri-Hi-Y Day, sponsored by the eighteen chapters in the Youngstown district, featured a new contest. In the afternoon area high school dance bands competed for a trophy donated by the *Vindicator*, and the winner was Niles McKinley. This competition became an annual event that lasted for years.

Minor league baseball in Youngstown ended in 1951. Playing for the Youngstown Athletics was Rudy York,

The miniature hook and ladder truck carried children on the midway.
RICK SHALE COLLECTION

Idora's fire truck was also used for promoting the park.
COURTESY OF HISTORIC IMAGES

1946 - 1954

Looking north toward the Wildcat's lift hill and modified first drop.
CHARLES J. JACQUES, JR. COLLECTION

the former Detroit Tiger veteran who had led the American League in home runs, RBI's, and slugging percentage in 1943. York would win the Middle American League home run title in 1951, his last year in professional baseball. But York's presence and even a special appearance at Idora by the legendary Cy Young, baseball's winningest pitcher, did not generate sufficient enthusiasm, and attendance averaged only one hundred fans per game. With the season still young and the team $7,000 in the red, owner Bill Koval announced that the franchise would shift to Oil City. In the previous season only 14,500 fans had come to watch the Youngstown Athletics. The *Vindicator* reported that "the radio and television competition of Cleveland games, high caliber sandlot ball, and Youngstown's low position in the M-A loop were contributory factors to the departure of the club."

America was at war in Korea, and patriotism was celebrated in several ways. Idora participated in Armed Forces Day on May 19, 1951. Army and Navy displays, including new weapons and vehicles, were set up in the park, and children received free jeep rides. The ROTC unit from Youngstown College performed marching drills for the crowd. On the Fourth of July, twenty-five veterans' organizations held a flag-burning ceremony at Idora. More than 3,500 torn and faded flags that had decorated veterans' graves since Memorial Day were properly disposed of in a memorial service at the ball field. More than 5,000 persons attended.

The *Vindicator* noted that in the post-war years the trend was away from company-wide picnics in favor of department picnics. Still, Idora was able to attract a number of bookings. The biggest, said Manager Rindin, would be the Babcock and Wilcox Tube Company of Beaver Falls, Pennsylvania, which usually drew 8,000 to 10,000.

On Monday, June 11, 1951, Charlie Deibel died at the age of 83. The retired chairman of the board of the Idora Amusement Company had been associated with the park for more than twenty-five years. His leadership had assured the park's survival during the Great Depression and World War II.

Shortly after noon on Sunday, December 9th, three months after the park had concluded its 1951 season, fire broke out in a storage building on the midway. Firefighters battled for three hours to keep the fire from spreading. Damages were estimated at $24,500 as 150 games and amusement devices, which were in storage, were destroyed.

The Youngstown Athletics had been unable to draw large crowds, but in

The brake run of the Wildcat was adjacent to the carousel building.
CHARLES J. JACQUES, JR. COLLECTION

A basement workshop and storage area were built under Heidelberg Gardens in the 1950s.
RICK SHALE COLLECTION

1946 - 1954

The Howdy Doody program ran on Youngstown's WFMJ-TV. Shortly after celebrating their 1,000th TV show, Howdy and his gang came to Idora and drew large crowds.
© THE VINDICATOR, 1999

August 1952 more than eight thousand people came to the Idora ball park for the annual Youth-On-Parade pageant. Children from Youngstown's twenty-two city playgrounds paraded in front of the grandstands with decorated doll buggies, bicycles, and wagons. Five women who worked as playground directors vied for the honor of queen of the pageant, which was sponsored by the City Park and Recreation Commission and the South Side Merchants & Civics Association.

No new rides had been added in 1952, but in 1953 Idora introduced the Hot Rods, a European-built car ride, which operated on a thousand-foot track. The outdoor roller skating rink continued to attract skaters.

In the ballroom Dan Ryan of WBBW Radio began to host record hops for the teen crowd. Dancing to records instead of live music was a relatively new phenomenon. When the fad began to catch on, some musicians saw the hops as a threat, and for a while the musicians' union insisted that Idora also provide a live band at the record hops. Dancing was scaled back to five nights a week, Wednesday through Sunday, in 1952 and 1953.

Near the end of the 1953 season the Howdy Doody gang visited Idora. The popular puppet had premiered in 1947 and quickly became a star of NBC television and radio. The show was carried Mondays through Fridays on WFMJ-TV.

Howdy, Buffalo Vic, Clarabell the Clown, Princess Summerfall Winterspring, and others made seven appearances on the weekend of September 5-6 and drew a huge crowd of appreciative young fans. (Buffalo Bob Smith was so busy doing the live television and radio shows that his brother Vic Smith often substituted for him at personal appearances.)

The Turtle, a modified tumble-bug ride that careened around a three hundred-foot circular, hilly track, was added in 1954. Like the Rocket Ships, it was manufactured by R. E. Chambers of Beaver Falls, Pennsylvania. Also added in 1954 were a hand car and tank for Kiddieland, bringing the ride total for children to fourteen.

Each ride or attraction at Idora had its own ticket. There was a Whip ticket, a Wildcat ticket, a carousel ticket, and so on. Since many of these attractions were owned by individual concessionaires, each operator sold tickets. This policy, dating from the park's earliest days, changed in 1954 when Idora adopted a universal ticket policy. Now patrons could buy a strip of tickets and use them on any ride or attraction. Major rides such as the Wildcat required three or four tickets while kiddie rides usually required only one. Children could get twelve kiddie rides for $1.00.

The Wildcat was the park's signature ride.
CHARLES J. JACQUES, JR. COLLECTION

1955 - 1959

7 THE BABY BOOM

Idora Park was changing dramatically. The closing of the swimming pool in 1949 followed by the decline in ballroom dancing meant that the park had to find new sources of revenue. As the baby boom generation grew in size and importance, this group would insure Idora's continued prosperity.

The high birth rates and good business conditions of the early 1950s were welcomed by the amusement park industry. By 1955 the baby boom generation was old enough to enjoy the park, and Idora finished the season with better than average profits despite a wet May and cold June.

The summer of 1955 was a watershed for the amusement park industry. On July 18, 1955, Walt Disney opened Disneyland, his new seventeen-million-dollar park in Anaheim, California. The opening had a dramatic effect on the whole amusement park industry because of Disney's television exposure. The country saw the park being built over national television, and its opening was one of the most anticipated events in the history of American popular entertainment. Kids in Youngstown saw the park open and began to dream of going to Disneyland some day.

Prior to Disneyland's opening, Idora was compared to amusement parks in eastern Ohio and western Pennsylvania. Even the best parks such as Euclid Beach Park in Cleveland and Kennywood Park in Pittsburgh were merely larger versions of Idora. They all had the same kind of rides, the same standards of cleanliness, and the same ambience. Disneyland changed all that. There was now a new national standard against which all amusement parks were measured. The parks that survived would be the ones that learned how to adapt to this new level Disney had established. Idora, with limited space for expansion and limited capital for improvements, did what it could to match the new standard.

To attract baby boomers the park added a miniature railroad named the "Little Erie." Idora's original bandstand, which in later years had been used as an aviary, was modified into a train loading station. The 4,500-foot railroad track ran past Kiddieland, the ball field, and the rear of the penny arcade as it circled the wooded hill on which stood the picnic shelters. The train could accommodate forty-eight passengers.

As the Big Band era waned, the park began to cut back on its dancing schedule. Up until 1949 Idora had offered dancing 7 nights a week. This was reduced to

The #20 bus to Idora Park on Youngstown's West Federal Street.
COURTESY OF HISTORIC IMAGES

Kiddieland opened in 1951.
CHARLES J. JACQUES, JR. COLLECTION

Pat Duffy, Jr. (left) and his father, Pat Duffy, Sr.
EDWARD C. LEARNER COLLECTION

6 nights in 1950 and 1951 and 5 nights in 1952 and 1953. In 1954 the dancing was cut to only 4 nights a week. By the mid-1950s Idora could no longer count on dancing as a steady source of revenue. Part of the strategy to attract teenagers and the college crowd was to remodel the dance pavilion, which was now forty-five years old. The old exterior decorations and the Moorish towers and cupolas were stripped away in 1955, and a new roof was installed. A new men's room was added inside with further interior changes scheduled for fall.

One institution that made extensive use of the ballroom in the mid-1950s was Youngstown University. The Snowflake Frolic, Mardi Gras dance, and Pete Penguin Ball were some of the events held annually at Idora for the college students.

The renovation of the dance pavilion's interior in 1956 concluded the two-year, $200,000 remodeling project. The new interior featured pastel colors, a low ceiling, and a $20,000 indirect lighting system with three-color neon. WFMJ-TV did two broadcasts from the ballroom to commemorate opening day. The first was a live telecast of a "Teen-Age Party," and the second was an evening broadcast of celebrity interviews and dancing to Hal McIntire's band. On June 9th WFMJ-TV broadcast *Rumpus Room* from the park, and on June 14th the station held a special Idora Day with the *Adelaide Snyder Show* in the morning, and a newscast, the *Hal's a Poppin* show, and *Kitchen Corner* with Marge Mariner in the afternoon.

The annual *Vindicator* Hi-Y and Tri-Hi-Y Day grew in popularity. An attendance record set in 1955 was broken in 1956 as fourteen thousand students showed up. Warren St. Mary's won the annual dance band contest for the second year in a row beating bands from South, Fitch, and Canfield High Schools.

The jitterbugs and bobby-soxers of the 1940s were beginning to give way to the rock and rollers of the 1950s. Every Friday was Teen-Age Night at the Idora

The ballroom's interior underwent a major renovation in 1956.
CHARLES J. JACQUES, JR. COLLECTION

1955 - 1959

The Old Mill and Falls were illuminated at night.
RICK SHALE COLLECTION

The donut stand at the park.
STELLA PARKS COLLECTION PROVIDED BY EDWARD C. LEARNER

ballroom. Hugh Johnston, another disc jockey from WBBW, had run the record hops in 1954 and 1955. He was followed by WHOT's Dick Biondi, who came to the area when WHOT went on the air in 1955. Biondi hosted the hops for a few years and later gained national fame as a disc jockey in Buffalo, Chicago, and Los Angeles.

Manager Max Rindin emphasized a firm policy on dress and behavior at the record hops. "Slacks, jeans, and shorts are not permitted on the floor," he warned. "'Wild and distasteful' dancing will not be tolerated." One could almost hear the echo of Manager Platt's edict against "fancy dancing" back in 1915.

Vindicator columnist Esther Hamilton wrote a lengthy profile of Max Rindin in 1956. He had come to Youngstown in 1925 and had gone to work for Charlie Deibel. He soon became Deibel's bookkeeper and right hand man. Rindin's first job at Idora was guessing weights, and from there he moved on to managing the refreshment stands. In the mid-1930s he became assistant manager and in 1941 general manager of the park. In 1949 Rindin also became part owner as well as general manager of Idora.

Idora Park had long been advertised as Youngstown's "Million Dollar Playground" because, as Esther Hamilton pointed out, "the equipment and grounds could not be replaced for that figure." In 1956 the park contained twenty-six rides, seven refreshment stands, and Heidelberg Gardens. The dance pavilion could hold six thousand people at one time, and the paved parking lot could accommodate three thousand cars. The park employed about 30 full time and 200 to 225 seasonal workers, and had a payroll of about $150,000.

Idora was often used as a site for political rallies by both the Republicans and

Democrats. On October 15, 1956, area Republicans packed the ballroom to hear Vice-President Richard Nixon deliver a campaign speech. He was accompanied by his wife Pat, Ohio's two Republican senators John Bricker and George Bender, and many other state and local leaders.

The *Vindicator* reported that by 1957 more people were coming to the park than had ten or fifteen years ago. The paper quoted park officials as saying there was a difference, however, in visitation patterns. "Families no longer bring their picnic baskets and stay for the day. They come for three or four hours, then leave and a new group takes their place." This trend meant that people were spending less money per visit than in prior years.

To entice more visitors, Idora announced that four brand new 1957 cars—three Plymouths and one De Soto—would be given away during the course of the season. A Skywheel and Tubs of Fun for Kiddieland were added, bringing the ride total for the park to twenty-eight. The Skywheel was a major, spectacular ride, which had two Ferris wheels located on the ends of long steel arms. Both the wheels and the arms rotated. At night the Skywheel was brightly lit.

Dancing prices were increased slightly. For the opening weekend the Friday night record hop cost fifty cents, the Saturday dance with the Glenn Ross Orchestra was $1.25, and the Sunday headliner with Woody Herman cost $2.00. Also appearing during the 1957 season were the Buddy Morrow, Ralph Marterie, Sam Donohue, and Tommy Carlyn bands.

A $5,000 fire caused some damage to Kiddieland during the off-season, but all was repaired by the time the 1958 season opened. No new rides were added, but a new midway was added to Kiddieland, and the picnic area was remodeled. Modernistic fronts were added to the carousel and the Jack Rabbit. The park adopted a weekends-only policy for April and went to a Tuesday-through-Sunday regular season schedule on May 9th.

Arizona Hopi Indian ceremonial dancers were engaged as an opening attraction. Buddy Lee and his Orchestra opened at the dance pavilion, with Les and Larry Elgart and their Orchestra

The tower of the Rocket Ship ride.
CHARLES J. JACQUES, JR. COLLECTION

The Jack Rabbit coaster featured open-front cars.
CHARLES J. JACQUES, JR. COLLECTION

1955 - 1959

The carousel included two ornately carved chariots.
RICK SHALE COLLECTION

Professional wrestling, boosted by television exposure, grew increasingly popular in the years following World War II, and Youngstown had its share of fans. In August an outdoor pro wrestling show was presented at the ball field. "Nature Boy" Buddy Rogers (Mr. America) took on Juan Sebastian, and 601-pound Country Boy Calhoon wrestled Jack Terry and Bill Scholl at the same time. The card included girl grapplers as well.

The many nationalities represented in Youngstown's population continued to sponsor ethnic days at Idora. Italian Day continued to draw one of the largest crowds. The anti-German sentiment of the war years had faded, and German Day (now called German-American Day to minimize any lingering wartime resentment) had been resurrected in 1955. The groups used their days to have fun at the park but also to celebrate their cultural heritage with folk dancing and singing and to discuss topics of concern. At the annual Hungarian Day in 1958, for example, the day's activities featured speeches praising the Hungarian freedom fighters and attacking the communists who had invaded the country in 1956.

Record hops were held every Friday. Youngstown police noted a marked rise in juvenile delinquency in the summer of 1958 and identified record hops as a source of the trouble. In August the Youngstown police issued strict guidelines for teen dances. The rules were aimed at dances held throughout the city, but of course the Idora hops were

playing for the Sunday Over-18 Friendship dance. Tickets were $1.50. Other bands playing in 1958 included Harry James, Sammy Kaye, and Kai Winding. In August Danny and the Juniors and the Poni-Tails headlined a summer dance party at the ballroom.

Youngstown University held many dances at Idora Park in the 1950s and 1960s.
RICK SHALE COLLECTION

affected. An 11 p.m. curfew was established, and all teens attending the hops had to carry parental permission slips. Sock hops were limited to those under fourteen, and record hops limited to those between the ages of fourteen and eighteen. Shorts, pedal pushers, T-shirts, and jeans were banned. The police also ordered that all hops had to be sponsored and supervised by legitimate organizations such as schools, churches, or clubs. A police matron was to be on duty in the girls' restroom. The *Vindicator* listed the additional rules: "The regulations ban hops in the downtown area and require adequate parking. Dance floors must be adequately lighted and prohibit in-and-out privileges. There will be no smoking on the premises, nor sale of intoxicating beverages."

The late 1950s were not only an era of juvenile delinquency but also the age of fallout shelters and fear of nuclear war. On August 31, 1958, Idora found itself under "atomic attack." A mock village was set up on the Idora ball field, and Civil Defense volunteers from over a dozen Ohio counties gathered at the park to stage a preparedness drill. Army and Air Force personnel also participated, and an Army Nike missile and other anti-aircraft weapons were brought to the park. These realistic props, said the *Vindicator*, "added to the drama as CD went into action on all phases of a bombing alert from the first warning through the explosion and post attack activities." An explosion was set off at 8:30 p.m. Saturday night signaling the attack, and some volunteers served as casualties. Radiation levels were checked, and police and fire officials took simulated emergency actions.

Youngstown University's 1957 Christmas Dance.
RICK SHALE COLLECTION

WFMJ-TV personality Susie Sidesaddle visits Idora.
COURTESY OF HISTORIC IMAGES

1955 - 1959

The crowd watches WFMJ-TV's live broadcast from Idora.
WFMJ-TV

Kirby Grant, star of NBC's Sky King, at Isaly's-WFMJ Family Day.
WFMJ-TV

The Isaly's-WFMJ Family Day was held each August, and in 1958 Martha Raye and the Kenley Players were guest stars. WFMJ-TV broadcast live from Idora from 1 p.m. to 7 p.m., and fans got to meet local television personalities Susie Sidesaddle and the Funhouse Gang, Captain Hal Fryar, and Marge Mariner. WFMJ Radio was also represented at the park that summer as Marc Howard hosted many of the record hops following Dick Biondi's departure.

The addition of the Round-Up, built by Hrubetz of Salem, Oregon, in 1959 brought the park's ride total to 29 (15 major rides and 14 Kiddieland rides). A new attraction did not always raise the ride total because older rides were generally retired without any publicity. The Round-Up was a spinning, circular ride that pinned the riders to the wall of the ride by centrifugal force as the wheel was elevated to a forty-five degree angle.

The antique carousel horses were repainted, and the parking lot was repaved for the season opener. The dance pavilion dress policy required teenage boys to wear dress slacks and girls to wear dresses or skirts and blouses. Men over eighteen

WFMJ-TV's Captain Hal Fryar entertains at Idora.
WFMJ-TV

had to wear a suit or sport jacket. Blue jeans and Bermudas were not permitted.

The Isaly's-WFMJ Family Day featured Sky King in person. The show aired nationally on NBC every afternoon. Actor Kirby Grant, who played Sky King, joined local WFMJ television personalities Susie Sidesaddle, Hal Fryar, and Marge Mariner to give away prizes and meet fans.

On September 27th Senator John F. Kennedy brought his 1960 presidential campaign to Idora's ballroom. He spoke to an enthusiastic crowd of 1,500 Democrats at a Roosevelt-Truman Dinner. Don L. Hanni, Jr. served as toastmaster, and Congressman Michael J. Kirwan introduced Kennedy, who received a key to the city from Mayor Frank Kryzan. Accompanying Senator Kennedy was his younger brother Edward Kennedy and U. S. Senator Stephen Young of Ohio. Virtually all Democratic office holders and office seekers from Youngstown were in attendance.

The armored horse on the carousel.
RICK SHALE COLLECTION

Vindicator *publisher William F. Maag, Jr.; Senator John F. Kennedy; and Congressman Mike Kirwan at Kennedy's presidential campaign dinner at Idora in 1959.*
DON HANNI, JR. COLLECTION

1960 - 1970

8 COMPETITION HEATS UP

Idora adapted to the changing demographics of the late 1950s. Kiddieland brought more families to the park, and the baby boomers grew old enough to be introduced to the park's adult rides. But while it was easy and relatively inexpensive to build a Kiddieland, it would prove much harder to add attractions such as new roller coasters or water rides that appealed to teenagers. Idora's inability to generate the cash flow necessary to replace old rides with an expensive, new generation of rides would make it more difficult each year for the park to compete.

As Idora entered the 1960s, new competition sprang up on all sides. The Interstate Highway system and the Ohio Turnpike made it easier to get to Idora, but these roads also made it easier for people in Idora's traditional market area to go elsewhere.

Cedar Point, located in Sandusky, Ohio, soon became Idora's biggest competitor. The Point, which had begun as a beach resort in 1870, reached its peak of popularity under the ownership and control of George Boeckling in the years from 1910 to 1930. Boeckling's death and the Great Depression led to Cedar Point's decline. Boeckling left his share of the park in trust, and no one was willing to make the changes that would have kept the park competitive.

While World War II revived Idora's business, the war merely continued the Point's downward slide. Cedar Point's infrastructure was so badly in need of repair that by the mid-1950s it looked as though the park would close. But the park was revitalized under the leadership of George Roose and Emile Legros. Starting slowly in 1958 and then with increasing speed, Cedar Point experienced a renaissance and became the premier amusement park in northern Ohio. With the new Ohio Turnpike even Youngstown was less than three hours away.

Picnics were responsible for more than half of Idora's annual revenue, and every picnic lost hurt the park's profit margin. Idora Park attempted to compete by adding new rides and booking well known entertainers. Two more rides were added in 1960: miniature hot rods and a "space age amusement" designed by Oarco of Columbus. Four cars carried sixteen passengers forty feet into the air. No other park in the country had this attraction. Park officials said the ride was so new it did not have a name, so a contest was begun to name it. Eddie Walker won the contest and named the new mystery ride The Orbit. This attraction lasted only a season or two at Idora.

Chief Featherman and Clarabell of the Howdy Doody Show along with young Tim Stanley at Idora, August 10, 1960.
TIM STANLEY COLLECTION

Dances had been a lucrative business for parks in the 1930s and 1940s, but by the 1950s interest in traditional ballroom dancing was all but dead. Most old-style orchestras were patronized by the over-forty crowd. Parks across the country searched for ways to attract a new generation. Idora's policy was to bring a name band for one night each week, and the 1960 schedule was impressive: among the headliners were Stan Kenton, Guy Lombardo, Maynard Ferguson, Dave Brubeck, Les Brown, and Louis Armstrong, who was making his first appearance at Idora in many years. Youngstown University student organizations continued to patronize the ballroom with Homecoming and Christmas Dances, the Engineer's Ball, Junior Prom, and the Inter-Fraternity Council Ball added to the list of college events held at Idora.

WHOT's Boots Bell served as disc jockey for the record hops. He replaced Frank Sweeney, who had run the hops the previous season. Boots Bell quickly became one of the area's top radio personalities, and the hops grew in popularity.

Despite the presence of a small park police force, Idora was not immune to occasional crime and vandalism. Early on the morning of Saturday, June 11, 1960, a gang of safecrackers overpowered Idora's night watchman and broke into the park's five safes. When Sam Boncilla, Idora's labor foreman with fifty years of service at the park, arrived for work, he found the guard handcuffed and taped to a chair in the park office. The park had had a big crowd Friday night, and the hooded thieves stole $20,000.

In July 1960 five Warren youths were arrested for "sudsing" the Rapids. Many people recall with some amusement seeing the Rapids fill with soapsuds, but in truth this "harmless prank" was a destructive act of vandalism. Manager Max Rindin said it was the third time in two years that vandals had thrown soap or detergent into the water ride. The circulating pump quickly churned the soap into giant suds that filled the channel and soon clogged the machinery. Thousands of gallons of water were needed to flush out the system. The youths were given suspended sentences, fined, and ordered to pay over $1,000 in damages. In August the Rapids suffered another sudsing; two out-of-town men were arrested and ordered to make restitution. The frequency of detergent vandalism diminished considerably when news of prosecution and fines was widely publicized. Science also came to the rescue. "Before that summer ended," said Max Rindin, "a major chemical company had developed a water additive that canceled the foaming action."

In August the Howdy Doody stars, who had first visited Idora in 1953, made a return appearance for Isaly's-WFMJ Family Day. Buffalo Vic, again subbing for his brother Buffalo Bob Smith, was joined by Clarabell, Chief Featherman, and Zippy the Chimp. The appearance was something of a swan song. Just six weeks after the Idora engagement, the *Howdy Doody Show* was cancelled after a thirteen-year run on NBC.

To try to build attendance, Idora presented something new each season. In 1961 the Flying Coaster was added as the park's thirty-first ride. Designed by Norman Bartlett of Miami, Florida, this ride followed a circular track, and the sudden up-and-down movements of the cars provided the thrills. The park was open six nights a week from 7 p.m. to midnight with dancing scheduled every night. Tuesdays were rock and roll, and

Mike Roncone Band in the ballroom in 1960.
MIKE RONCONE COLLECTION

Youngstown radio personality Boots Bell, who ran Idora's record hops.
CAROL W. BELL COLLECTION

The 1961 Miss Teenage Youngstown pageant was held in the ballroom.
GAIL THOMAS MINNEMAN COLLECTION

1960 - 1970

The Idora Limited and Kiddieland circa 1960.
CHARLES J. JACQUES, JR. COLLECTION

Doing the Bunny Hop at Youngstown University's 1961 Snowflake Frolic held in Idora's ballroom.
RICK SHALE COLLECTION

The Flying Cages were located in front of Heidelberg Gardens.
EDWARD C. LEARNER COLLECTION

Wednesdays were for the name bands. Thursdays were for the Over 29 Club, which transferred from the Elms Ballroom to Idora. Friday nights were for the record hops, Saturdays were for couples only, and Sundays were the friendship dances, stag only. The same schedule was used in 1962.

On October 7, 1961, the local Miss Teenage America contest was held at the Idora ballroom. WHOT's George Barry was master of ceremonies, and recording star Joe Dowell provided the vocals. Gail Thomas from Boardman High School was crowned Miss Teenage Youngstown. The runner-up court included Elaine Lowry of Hubbard, Sandy Vasu of Boardman, Ruth Bartholomew of Hubbard, and Becky Johnson of Austintown Fitch High School.

Idora opened the 1962 season with five new rides including two major rides built in Europe—a German Wild Mouse and Roto-Jet. The Wilde Maus, as Idora spelled it, was a small coaster with individual cars making sharp turns on a steel track. It featured hairpin curves and short, choppy hills. The absence of catwalks or guard rails gave the riders a risky feeling of being on the edge. The Roto-Jet, also from Germany, allowed passengers in the eight planes to raise or lower their vehicle during the flight. It was one of the new generation of rides operated by hydraulics. These rides required more technical expertise to maintain and were much more expensive to operate.

Also added were the Flying Cages, a decidedly low-tech attraction that required riders to rock or pump the cages back and forth to get them to soar over a bar. New to Kiddieland were an outboard speedboat ride and a kiddie turnpike where electric cars followed a track over hills and curves.

In June the U. S. Army Field Band came to Idora, and a crowd of three thousand heard the one hundred-piece orchestra perform at the Idora ball field. Boardman High School students served as usherettes for the concert.

In September former president Harry S. Truman came to Idora and entertained a crowd of two thousand with

a rousing political address. Longtime congressman Mike Kirwan joined Truman in roasting the Republicans. Other dignitaries included Governor David Lawrence of Pennsylvania, Governor Mike DiSalle of Ohio, U.S. Senator Stephen Young, and Carl Weygandt, Chief Justice of the Ohio Supreme Court.

The late 1950s and early 1960s were the heyday of the television westerns with shows such as *Bonanza*, *Cheyenne*, *Maverick*, and *Gunsmoke*, and this trend began to affect Idora. In 1962 the park added to the midway a talking, gunslinging cowboy robot that challenged park patrons to a western duel with cork guns. In 1963 the park's dark ride was re-themed and called The Gold Nugget. Visitors toured the Old West in gold mine cars with barrel engines. The attraction was a western version of the old haunted house ride. The re-theming was done by Bill Tracey of Outdoor Dimensional Display Company in New Jersey. Tracey specialized in dark ride displays, animation, re-theming fronts, and fiberglass figures. His work evoked responses ranging from laughter to sheer horror. He designed dark rides and fun houses all over America including Elitch Gardens in Denver; Dorney Park in Allentown, Pennsylvania; Hunt's Pier in Wildwood, New Jersey; and Trimpers in Ocean City, Maryland.

Tragedy again struck the park on July 16, 1963, as sixteen-year-old Richard Nelson of New Castle was killed while riding the Jack Rabbit. When the ride began, witnesses said the teenager had climbed out of the car and had run up the catwalk alongside the coaster as it was pulled up the chainlift. He climbed back in the front car but continued to clown around. One witness said "the Nelson youth at one point stood up in the car and turned around facing the others as the cars raced around curves and down dips." Finally the ride's momentum hurled the youth out of the car, and he fell to his death. Manager Max Rindin said it was the park's first fatality since a person had been killed on the Wildcat in 1948. Coroner Dr. Nathan Belinky ruled the death accidental and said it was caused by the youth's own actions.

The 1964 season opened on May 15th, and among the new attractions were a thrill ride called the Trabant and a new replica of the 1863 C. P. Huntington train built by Chance Manufacturing, Wichita, Kansas. This miniature train, named for the nineteenth-century railroad magnate who co-founded the Central Pacific and Southern Pacific Railroads, would be a fixture in the park for the next twenty years. The Orbit returned to the park after a few years' absence but again did not last long. The miniature golf course underwent a $25,000 renovation. A *Vindicator* editorial stressed the importance of the park as a "summertime industry" and noted "Idora won't compete with the World's Fair in New York but it won't cost as much either."

For 1964 Idora continued to use both name bands and record hops to generate ballroom business. Among the bands booked for the 1964 season were Guy Lombardo, Artie Arnell, Si Zentner, and Bobby Dale. The Over 29 Club dances continued, and for the next decade Rita Baytos offered weekly lessons in the waltz, tango, fox-trot, jitterbug, and other steps. The first record hop of the season featured the El Dorados with Boots Bell as the disc jockey. Admission was fifty cents. This was the first season for dancing in the Kove South located in Heidelberg Gardens. The Kove dances originated on the second floor of the Elms Ballroom, owned by Tony Cavalier. The Elms was located on Youngstown's north side near the Youngstown University

Candy Floss stand.
TAMMI WALSH COLLECTION

Rocket Ship ride on the upper midway.
RICK SHALE COLLECTION

Idora's Fun House 1963.
CHARLES J. JACQUES, JR. COLLECTION

1960 - 1970

Mike Roncone (center) and Youngstown's own Human Beingz.
MIKE RONCONE COLLECTION

Kove South dancing.
MIKE RONCONE COLLECTION

campus. When the dances, aimed at the 17-to-23 year-old college crowd, became popular, they were also held one night a week at Idora, and the "Kove South" was born. Mike Roncone's Orchestra provided the music, and casual dress was permitted. Unlike the record hops in the Idora ballroom, the Kove dances featured live music exclusively. "We played everything that was high-power dancing," said Roncone.

The presidential election year again brought a parade of politicians to Idora. Senator Hubert H. Humphrey, the Democratic vice-presidential candidate, addressed a Labor Day rally. The following day Congressman Robert A. Taft, Jr. also visited Idora to promote his campaign for a U.S. Senate seat. In early October Sargent Shriver, the Director of the Peace Corps, spoke at a Democratic fund-raiser, and two weeks later Senator Barry Goldwater brought his presidential campaign to the Idora ballroom.

Pat Duffy, Sr. retired as Idora's president in 1965. He was named chairman of the board, and Tony Cavalier became the new park president. Also retiring in 1965 was Doris Turney, who owned the cotton candy stand. She had come to Idora in the mid-1930s and had sold candy floss, as it was then called, first near the ballroom and later under the Rocket Ships, where her grandson Chuck Anderson and great-granddaughter Tammi Walsh would operate the concession until the park closed.

In September Cavalier's Elms Ballroom was torn down, and many events previously scheduled there were shifted to Idora. One memorable event of the season was the appearance of James Brown, the godfather of soul, at Idora's ballroom.

The 1966 season offered a few new attractions: an illusion-type ride called Over the Falls and some junior hot rods imported from Germany. Porky the Paper-Eater also arrived in 1966 and would remain a fixture at the park until its closing. Porky, a talking trash receptacle, was housed in a giant mushroom.

On December 1, 1966, Patrick Duffy, Sr. died at the age of eighty-seven. He had been associated with the park for sixty-one years. Duffy began his career at Idora in 1905 by operating several games and refreshment stands; when Rex Billings and Charles Deibel took over the park in 1924, Duffy had the concessions for all the games and several rides. In 1949 Duffy, along with Tony Cavalier and Max Rindin, acquired control of the park. Duffy was elected President and retained that office for sixteen years until he was elevated to chairman.

Walt Disney died the same month as Pat Duffy, Sr. By the time Disney died, Disneyland had become a truly national park. Before his death Disney set in motion plans to build a second major park, Walt Disney World in Orlando, Florida, which opened on October 1, 1971. It was much larger than Disneyland and offered more attractions, and its location on the east coast exposed even more people from eastern Ohio and western Pennsylvania to Disney's Magic Kingdom.

After a visit to Walt Disney World, a picnic at Idora seemed almost quaint and old fashioned. Idora's grounds were small and not as spotless as Disney's parks. There were no themes or costumed employees, and the rides, except for the coasters and the mill chute, were little more than carnival attractions.

It became increasingly hard for Idora to compete. Spectacular rides like the Wildcat now cost close to a million dollars, and the park's revenues could not justify the purchase of another coaster or other major ride attraction.

The highlight of the 1967 season was a new ride called the Paratrooper, manufactured by Hrubetz of Salem, Oregon. The ballroom was also refurbished, and new mercury vapor lighting was installed in the parking areas. Foreshadowing a policy that would eventually become standard, Idora inaugurated a POP or Pay-One-Price policy for holidays and special occasions. The first use of the new policy was on Memorial Day; children 12 and under were admitted for $1.25, and adults paid $2.50. The record hop season began with a concert by Sam the Sham and the Pharaohs. Mike Roncone's band continued to provide fast-tempo dance music at the Kove South in Heidelberg Gardens. Local favorites such as the Human Beingz and Phil Keaggy also played at the Kove.

Only a few days after the park opened, a disturbance resulted in the arrest of two men for inciting a riot. The men reportedly goaded a large crowd by shouting "Black Power" and "Kill the Police"; nine police cruisers were needed to disperse a crowd of five hundred youths. In the weeks that followed, the park suffered a loss of attendance. On May 27, 1967, the *Vindicator* called for community support. Idora, noted the editorial, "is, actually, a business which merits support from all Youngstown people. It is a two-million-dollar enterprise with a daily payroll of $1,400–six days a week–during the four summer months and, obviously, contributes a sizable chunk of revenue in taxes." The editorial added: "A few wayward teenagers should not be allowed to destroy the area's usefulness and, obviously, rumors without substantial basis should be disregarded."

Idora was not the only park to suffer from social disturbances, and amusement parks around the country were forced to review their admission policies. Park owners discovered that a modest admission charge in addition to ride tickets tended to keep out many of the troublemakers. Other owners who were unable or unwilling to cope with the racial and social unrest of the times closed their doors and sold the property to developers. Euclid Beach Park in Cleveland closed in 1969, and Meyers Lake Park in Canton closed in 1973.

In August 1967 the first Penn-Ohio Polka Festival was held at Idora. Larry Walk organized the event, which featured several bands performing for twelve continuous hours. Part of the festival was broadcast on Larry Walk's *Happy Polkaland* radio show. This was one of the first major polka festivals in the country, and it was so successful that Idora asked that it be a regular feature. Walk would produce several festivals each summer at the park for the next eighteen years.

Both the Fun House and the Rapids underwent transformations by Bill Tracey of Outdoor Dimensions for the 1968 season. Tracey was one of the greatest fun house artists of the 1960s, and he transformed the old Fun House into the Whacky Shack, described by the *Vindicator* as "a psychedelic-type fun house which features strobe lighting, high frequency floors, 'a tipsy room,' and many other challenges in the mod mood."

The Rapids was re-themed and became The Lost River with the familiar mill chute ride now labeled a jungle cruise. The Old Mill was converted to a jungle hut, and an elephant was installed above the entrance as ballyhoo for the new theme. Tracey also created Lost

Talking trash receptacle.
RICK SHALE COLLECTION

The Jack Rabbit's cupola and first drop.
CHARLES J. JACQUES, JR. COLLECTION

1960 - 1970

Idora's Ferris Wheel.
RICK SHALE COLLECTION

The Rapids ride was re-themed into the Lost River.
CHARLES J. JACQUES, JR. COLLECTION

Game and food stands on the lower midway.
MAHONING VALLEY HISTORICAL SOCIETY

River rides at Hershey Park in Hershey, Pennsylvania, and Paragon Park in Nantasket, Massachusetts. A thrill ride called the Skydiver by Chance Manufacturing, Wichita, Kansas, was also added, but it proved disappointing and Manager Max Rindin put it up for sale after only a season. Go-Go clowns entertained visitors on the midway every Sunday.

Idora continued to offer a very wide variety of music. The ballroom offered teen dances with both live bands and record hops as well as a regular schedule of orchestras for adult dancing. Tickets for Guy Lombardo in 1968 were $4.00 in advance, $4.50 at the door. On Sundays and special days the Idora Dixieland Band played on the midway on a float bandstand. Polka music continued to gain in popularity, and on Slovak Day the park hosted the Penn-Ohio Polka Festival with Happy Louie, Stanky and the Coal Miners, the Polka Jets, and the Jolly J's. The park also offered three free jazz concerts.

In 1968 Idora offered a variety of ticket plans. Tuesdays and Thursdays were Family Bargain Days with prices reduced to fifteen cents for major rides and ten cents for the kiddie rides. The pay-one-price admission, used for holidays, was raised to $3.00. On July 4th, for example, a visitor had the following choices: for $3.00 one could ride all day, for $2.50 one could purchase a ride book good for 10 adult rides or 20 kiddie rides, or for $1.00 one could gain admission to the park and buy universal ride tickets.

The end of summer did not mean the end of all activities at the Park. Some social events continued during the winter months. On New Year's Eve, for instance, the park sponsored two dances: in the ballroom the Artie Arnell Orchestra entertained for $10.00 a couple, and in Heidelberg Gardens Wally's Polka Chips played for $6.00 a couple.

As the decade neared its end, Idora faced increased competition as nearby parks made the changes necessary to survive the period. In 1968 Kennywood Park built the Thunderbolt, the first coaster in the region that was of the same quality as Idora's Wildcat. Until then, only a few coasters in the country were as good as the Wildcat, and none of them was located in eastern Ohio or western Pennsylvania.

In 1969 a group of young executives left Cedar Point to take over Geauga Lake in Aurora, Ohio. This park had been in a decline since World War II. Nothing new had been added, and the only rides of significance were a John A. Miller coaster that was badly in need of repair and an Illions carousel. By the end of the 1960s Geauga Lake was almost moribund. The new owners quickly built a monorail, sky tower, and a corkscrew coaster (one of the first) and started competing directly with Idora for group and picnic business in northeastern Ohio.

Geauga Lake's new management team then compounded Idora's problem by selling part of their lake frontage to Sea World, which built Sea World of Ohio. Although Sea World was not an amusement park, it was stiff competition for Idora and other parks for summertime recreation dollars. Geauga Lake and Sea World were only ninety minutes away from Youngstown.

In 1969 Idora operated 14 major and 14 kiddie rides. The park tried more theming and replaced the German hot rods with the Hooterville Highway, which featured antique cars. The TV shows *Petticoat Junction*, which premiered in 1963, and *Green Acres*, which began in 1965, were both set in bucolic Hooterville, so the name of the new attraction would have been familiar to a television generation.

By the late 1960s the park had fallen into a familiar pattern: Idora opened in

Lee Castle and the Jimmy Dorsey Orchestra.
RICK SHALE COLLECTION

Dancing in the ballroom.
CHARLES J. JACQUES, JR. COLLECTION

A jungle hut and palm trees decorated the Lost River ride.
MAHONING VALLEY HISTORICAL SOCIETY

Tilt-A-Whirl at night.
RICK SHALE COLLECTION

early May for weekends only and went to its regular six-day-a-week summer schedule after Memorial Day. The kick-off event was the annual *Vindicator* Hi-Y-Tri-Hi-Y Play Day and dance band contest. Guy Lombardo returned each season to headline a list of big bands. Over 21 dances were held on Fridays, and the Over 29 Club met once a week. The Penn-Ohio Polka Festivals were held in June and August.

For the 1970 season Idora Park made special plans to celebrate its seventy-fifth anniversary. The only thing overlooked, apparently, was accuracy, for in truth, this was only the park's seventy-first anniversary. No one seemed to remember when the park had been founded, so on June 17, 1970, ceremonies at City Hall honored the park's Diamond Anniversary. Mayor Jack Hunter offered congratulations to Max Rindin, Idora's general manager, and City Council passed a resolution commending the park as "a place for good, clean, wholesome fun for families in this community."

Idora employed about 150 people that summer who were dressed for the first time in jackets and smocks. The Challenger Parachuting team came to the park, and their feats recalled the daredevil balloon aerialists of Idora's early seasons. Less nostalgic and more controversial was a July 4th rodeo, the first in many years at the park. Prompted by complaints over inhumane devices such as flank straps, Common Pleas Judge Clyde Osborne issued an injunction to halt the show. The rodeo owner and promoter defied the court order and held the event anyway. They were convicted and fined for contempt of court.

Recording artist Bobby Sherman gave two performances on August 19th for WHOT Day and drew seven thousand fans, one of the largest crowds in years. The Penn-Ohio Polka Festival also drew huge crowds, and Buddy Rich, "the world's greatest drummer," had two sell-out performances.

The anniversary season concluded with the traditional Labor Day "Final Fling" festivities. Sunday was Family Bargain Day with rides priced at 10 cents and 15 cents. Labor Day featured $3.50 ride-all-day tickets. The season was quite successful, and the park claimed an attendance record of more than 750,000 visitors.

1971 - 1980

9 SEARCHING FOR A STRATEGY

Idora Park spent the 1970s looking for ways to compete with Cedar Point, Geauga Lake, Kennywood, and Conneaut Lake Park. As the decade progressed, these competing parks spent more money, installed more spectacular rides, and became stronger economically, making Idora's attempts to retain and attract customers even more difficult.

Idora continued to make improvements and spent $150,000 to ready the park for the 1971 season. The old Auto Skooter bumper car ride was remodeled and became Helter Skelter, the name reflecting the new policy of allowing the drivers to travel in any direction. The Turbo from Chance Manufacturing, Wichita, Kansas, and the Scrambler, made by Eli Bridge, also made their debut. Idora also hosted several special events such as a sports and recreation

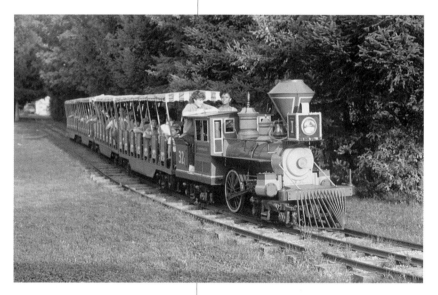

The C. P. Huntington train.
RICK SHALE COLLECTION

Fun on the Tilt-A-Whirl.
© THE VINDICATOR, 1999

show in May and an antique car show in July. To attract more picnic groups, Idora added a new picnic shelter that could accommodate 750 picnickers.

In 1972 the park added the Monster, a thrill ride made by Eyerly Aircraft, Salem, Oregon, and the Kooky Castle. The latter was a dark ride located next to the Fun House in the northwest corner of the park, the latest in a series of dark rides to occupy that location. Re-theming was a common practice in the amusement park industry. The mechanics of the ride and the building's structure would remain the same, but a new facade would signal a shift from a haunted house to a western town or a medieval castle. The cars would be redesigned, and the scary things that accosted riders in the dark would be changed.

The pay-one-price jumped to $4.00 for the 1972 season. In August the Clyde Beatty-Cole Bros. Circus came to Idora, but when the big trucks pulled into the park they found they could not get through the narrow gate into the ball field. The problem was solved by pitching the circus tent on the parking lot and parking cars on the ball field.

Presidential politics again made its presence felt in October when a rally for presidential candidate George McGovern was held at the Idora ballroom. The candidate did not attend but the main speaker

(Top) Kooky Castle, the park's dark ride.
PHOTOGRAPH BY CHARLES J. JACQUES, JR.

(Above) Idorables on the Rocket Ship ride.
MAHONING VALLEY HISTORICAL SOCIETY

Lost River splashdown.
CHARLES J. JACQUES, JR. COLLECTION

1971 - 1980

Caterpillar, Tilt-A-Whirl, and Rocket Ship rides on the upper midway.
PHOTOGRAPH BY CHARLES J. JACQUES, JR.

The Cheyenne Shootout was constructed in 1974.
© THE VINDICATOR, 1999

was Lawrence O'Brien, the Democratic National Campaign chairman. Former astronaut John Glenn (who would be elected to the U. S. Senate in 1974) and Representative Charles Carney also attended.

In 1973 the park opened on Easter Sunday, April 22nd, the earliest opening in years. To inaugurate the season the Easter bunny parachuted into the park. Unseasonably cold weather cut the usual crowd of 10,000-14,000 down to 4,000 for *Vindicator* Hi-Y-Tri-Hi-Y Day. In an attempt to draw a different crowd to Idora, WNIO Radio sponsored a Country Music Day with appearances by Roy Clark, Billy "Crash" Craddock, and others, but the country acts proved to be less popular at Idora than the Polka Festivals or the rock stars who came for WHOT's Hot Day.

Hoping to spark new interest and reclaim past visitors, the park owners chose the slogan "Rediscover Idora" to reflect a $250,000 renovation to ready the park for the 1974 season. For decades visitors to Idora had entered at a gate between the ballroom and the Jack Rabbit. A new ticket entrance was constructed at the south end of the ballroom and a new admission policy was begun. The pay-one-price policy, used since 1967 for holidays and special occasions, was extended to a daily policy. Individual ride tickets could still be purchased, but the park began for the first time to charge a small general admission fee. General manager Pat Duffy, Jr. told the Cleveland *Plain Dealer*, "We were pressured by our steady customers to follow the lead of the big new parks with their one-charge ride-all-day admission ticket and non-ride general admission." The end of free access to the park drew criticism, but as Duffy noted, "we got rid of the loafers, of the gangs of hoodlums who made the place uncomfortable for a family trade."

The midway had a new major attraction with the Cheyenne Shootout, a Western-themed electronic shooting gallery. It would anchor the south end of the midway until the park closed. The changes also included two new rides: the Spider by Eyerly and the Yo-Yo by Chance Manufacturing. Both offered a higher ride capacity. The Spider could accommodate 650 riders per hour, and the Yo-Yo could accommodate 800, double the capacity of the Kooky Castle or Paratrooper. Ride capacity per hour was an important consideration for park owners. No one liked to stand in a slow-moving line, and management knew that a customer standing in a line represented a customer who was not spending money on refreshments or games.

On February 6, 1975, the U. S. Department of Interior placed the Idora carousel on the National Register of Historic Places, an honor that only a few parks were given. All of the carousel horses were repaired and repainted. The park opened for weekends-only on the last Sunday in April and went to a Tuesday-to-Sunday schedule in mid-June. In July the Al Koran Shrine Circus opened a three-day engagement at Idora, and in August the Monkees performed for WHOT Day.

The Ridora ticket, as the all-day unlimited ride policy was called, remained at $4.00 for the fifth consecutive year, but senior citizens got a discount as did students with good report cards. The park also inaugurated a Senior Citizen Day. The Rock-O-Plane, another ride from Eyerly Aircraft, was added in 1976. To reflect America's Bicentennial, the carousel exterior was painted red, white, and blue. Stan Kenton played at the Bicentennial Ball on July 3rd as part of Youngstown's bicentennial activities. Other band bookings for the 1976 season included Guy Lombardo, Les Brown and his Band of Renown, Buddy Rich and Maynard Ferguson, and the orchestras of Tommy Dorsey and Glenn Miller.

Maintaining the park was expensive. Pat Duffy told *Vindicator* reporter Janie Jenkins that between $15,000 and $20,000 in lumber was replaced on the Wildcat each year and that it took eight

Idora's historic carousel.
PHOTOGRAPH BY CHARLES J. JACQUES, JR.

The Wildcat's track crossed over itself.
PHOTOGRAPH BY CHUCK WLODARCZYK

A solo passenger on the Kiddie Coaster.
© THE VINDICATOR, 1999

1971 - 1980

Bay City Rollers fans at Idora.
© THE VINDICATOR, 1999

men three and a half months to paint it. Though the park owners sometimes hired outside contractors to do major re-theming, they more often relied on their own staff. Victor Kosa served as the park's decorator for years and produced scenic effects for many attractions including dark rides and the columns and bandstand in the ballroom.

Admission prices crept upward: after holding steady at $4.00 for the past five years, the Ridora all-day ticket jumped to $4.75 in 1977. After 5 p.m. the price dropped to $3.75. The admission for those wishing to buy individual ride tickets was $1.50.

The Bay City Rollers, a rock group from Scotland, were the headliners for the annual WHOT Day. They drew an enthusiastic crowd, but the group's threats to cut the concert short and insufficient crowd control caused confusion. The group's handlers reneged on earlier promises of media access to the singers and treated the press rudely, prompting the *Vindicator* reporter to call the concert "chaotic and third-rate."

In 1978 Idora put an antique Fly-O-Plane (Flying Scooter) in the northeast corner of the park inside the track of the Hooterville Highway. The ride was purchased from West View Park in Pittsburgh, which closed in 1977. "We've lost a lot of competitors in the area," said Duffy. "That means more picnics for us." Duffy estimated that about 60 percent of their business would come from company bookings.

The major parks such as Cedar Point, Geauga Lake, and Kings Island in Ohio and nearby Kennywood Park in Pittsburgh continued to draw some of Idora's customers, yet Pat Duffy saw some good in their rivalry. "The big parks have been a good thing for us. They woke us up to cleanliness and variety. We've also had to learn how to go out and market our product."

One marketing device created in 1978 was the Idorables, three employees costumed as a chipmunk, a bunny, and a rooster. They wandered up and down the midway greeting customers, posing for pictures, and giving hugs to the children.

The pay-one-price remained at $4.75 for a second year, and the park also sold ten-cent ride tickets in $1.50 strips. Rides required three to six tickets, and corporations such as Pepsi, Amoco, and Burger

The Idorables were the park's costumed characters.
CHARLES J. JACQUES, JR. COLLECTION

A crowded day at the park.
© THE VINDICATOR, 1999

A ride on the wild side.
© THE VINDICATOR, 1999

The park adopted uniforms in the 1970s.
RICK SHALE COLLECTION

A high school band marches through the park.
CHARLES J. JACQUES, JR. COLLECTION

Chef offered discount promotions. Special days on the 1978 schedule included the hot rod show, antique auto show, six Sunday polka festivals, and Oktoberfest.

By the late 1970s roller coaster fever was sweeping the country. A 1974 *New York Times* article by Robert Cartmell, "The Quest for the Ultimate Roller Coaster," seems to have been a catalyst for the resurgence of the popular ride. Suddenly many parks were building new coasters, and older coasters were being judged and compared. The American Coaster Enthusiasts ranked the Idora Wildcat among the top ten coasters in the country. Allen Ambrosini, writing in *Ohio Magazine*, felt the Wildcat was the second best coaster in Ohio, outranked only by the Beast, recently built at Kings Island. He also placed the Jack Rabbit among Ohio's top ten coasters. This national and state-wide recognition gave Idora some much-needed publicity.

Publicity, however, did not always translate into profits, and events outside of Idora's control would soon threaten the park's revenues. In the Mahoning Valley September 19, 1977, is known as Black Monday. On that date the Youngstown Sheet and Tube Company, controlled by the Lykes Corporation, announced that it would close the

1971 - 1980

The park entrance sign on Billingsgate.
© THE VINDICATOR, 1999

Enjoying French fries was an Idora tradition.
PHOTOGRAPHS ©THE VINDICATOR, 1999

Campbell Works. Five thousand steelworkers lost their jobs. Fifteen months later the company closed the Brier Hill Works, and another thousand became unemployed. The closings hurt the local economy and caused a further fall off in park patronage. For many years Youngstown Sheet and Tube's annual outing had been Idora's largest picnic.

The 1978 season had been very successful with net profits up over 60 percent, but with the Mahoning Valley's economy worsening, Idora began to experience some financial reverses. Sales and gross profits fell, and expenses rose. Idora operated on a fiscal year that ran from May 1st to April 30th, and the balance sheet ending April 30, 1980, showed a net profit of $78,059, less than half the net profits of the previous year. Unemployment rates in the valley reached double digits.

The summer of 1980 provided no financial relief. Rain fell on 42 percent of the weekends that the park was open, and Idora's net profits fell another 26 percent. Fewer visitors came to the park because there were fewer people in the city. Youngstown's population dropped from 166,689 people in 1960 to 140,909 in 1970 and 115,436 in 1980, a decline of over 50,000 in just two decades.

The park adjoined a residential neighborhood.
CHARLES J. JACQUES, JR. COLLECTION

The polka festivals continued to draw crowds. Larry Walk promoted four festivals in 1980, bringing stars such as Marion Lush, Happy Louie, and Eddie Blazonczyk to Idora. Chartered buses brought polka fans from Cleveland, Toledo, Buffalo, Pittsburgh, Erie, and Johnstown.

Idora continued to be used occasionally for other purposes. In the spring of 1980 Senator Edward Kennedy, then campaigning for the Democratic presidential nomination, came to Idora and spoke from the same stage his brother, John F. Kennedy, had campaigned from in 1959.

In November 1980, a Hollywood film crew used Idora to shoot some scenes for *All the Marbles*, a comedy starring Peter Falk. Director Robert Aldrich hired over two hundred area residents to work as extras in the film.

Idora's miniature golf course included a windmill, Eiffel tower, and clown face.
PHOTOGRAPH BY CHARLES J. JACQUES, JR.

1981 - 1984

10 | GOING DOWNHILL FAST

A trainload of roller coaster fans.
PHOTOGRAPH BY CHARLES J. JACQUES, JR.

Rides on the upper midway.
PHOTOGRAPH BY CHARLES J. JACQUES, JR.

In 1981 Idora lost two of the most important figures in its history. Rex Billings, former owner and manager of the park, died April 20, 1981. Billings had managed Idora during the park's greatest period of expansion in the 1920s. He was credited with introducing three-cent kiddie days to the amusement park industry, and many of his ideas were copied by other parks.

Lillian Desmonde also died in 1981 at the age of 88. Though she had been gone from Youngstown for almost half a century, many old-timers could recall her theatrical career on the Idora stage and the pleasure she had given, and the *Vindicator* published an affectionate editorial eulogizing the actress.

The admission policy was again modified in 1981. The pay-one-price rose slightly from $5.50 to $5.95. General admission for those not wishing to ride was $2.00, and $3.00 would buy admission plus ten ride tickets. The biggest change was in the operating schedule. "After much soul searching," said Duffy, the park switched from a 6-day to a 4-day operating schedule. Most parks operated on 7-day weeks, and the reduced schedule was a sign of Idora's weakening situation. Idora now operated Thursday through Sunday. The out-of-town picnic business was up, and that took up some of the slack from the weakened local market.

Visitors were greeted by some very visible changes. The old Heidelberg Gardens was remodeled, given a western theme, and renamed the Crazy Horse Saloon. New also was a miniature lake set up in front of the Saloon that held remote-controlled miniature boats in less than a foot of water.

Amusement Business, a trade publication, reported that while business was down for many Ohio parks in 1981, attendance at Idora was up about 10 percent over the previous summer. Unfortunately, the increase did not reverse the downwardly spiraling net profits, which fell 45 percent. In just three years the net profits had dropped 80 percent.

In 1982 the unemployment rate in the Youngstown-Warren area peaked at 19.7 percent with over 46,000 people out of work. Faced with declining profits, the park owners again increased the admission price with the ride-all-day ticket now set at $6.95. Despite the decreased operating days and price increase, Idora drew 225,000 visitors in 1981 and 220,000 in 1982. Duffy dismissed the 5,000-person decline as insignificant. "That number could be made up in one day," he explained. But rumors began to circulate about Idora's future.

In October 1982 Pat Duffy, Jr., Max Rindin, and Leonard Cavalier put the park up for sale. The asking price was $1.5 million. Long hours, bad weather, and an uncertain economy were reasons given by the owners, who said they would continue to operate the park if there were no takers.

A Vindicator editorial noted that "When a company is put up for sale these days, the first guess is that business is bad, and it is near the end of the line. Fortunately, Idora Park is the exception."

By spring 1983, no buyers had been found, and the owners opened Idora for business as usual on a Thursday-to-Sunday schedule with Ridora ticket prices again set at $6.95. Thursdays offered free admission with ride tickets available for ten cents each. Most attractions required

The fun house was remodeled a final time into Laffin' Lena's Loonyland.
PHOTOGRAPH BY CHARLES J. JACQUES, JR.

The south turn of the Wildcat.
PHOTOGRAPH BY CHARLES J. JACQUES, JR.

1981 - 1984

The Hooterville Highway antique cars.
PHOTOGRAPH BY CHARLES J. JACQUES, JR.

The Fantastic Flying Machine, the park's Flying Scooter ride.
CHARLES J. JACQUES, JR. COLLECTION

Kiddieland car.
PHOTOGRAPH BY CHARLES J. JACQUES, JR.

The Spider with the Rock-O-Plane in the background.
CHARLES J. JACQUES, JR. COLLECTION

two to six tickets. Several promotions were used in the 1983 season: Carload Days (where a car full of people would be charged ten dollars), Two-For-One Days, and Old Fashioned Days. To counter the recent drop in attendance, Idora increased its advertising budget by 10 percent. *Amusement Business* reported that Idora extended its advertising campaign to Cleveland and Pittsburgh.

What did Idora Park look like in 1983, the last season before the fire? After entering the gate at the south end of the ballroom a visitor immediately encounters the Rock-O-Plane, Spider, and Yo-Yo set against a backdrop of tall trees in adjacent Mill Creek Park. Turning north and heading for the midway, one passes the ballroom on the right and miniature golf course and Turtle ride on the left.

At the north end of the ballroom one can turn right toward the Jack Rabbit coaster and ball field or head left to the Lost River ride. Newcomers will no doubt linger for a moment to watch the Lost River boats splash down in front of the cascading waterfall.

The midway stretches ahead with the park office on the west or left side followed by the Fascination parlor, Skee ball, the shooting gallery with live ammunition, and the popcorn stand. On the east side of the midway are the Cheyenne

The upper midway was crowded with attractions.
MAHONING VALLEY HISTORICAL SOCIETY

Antique car on the Hooterville Highway.
MAHONING VALLEY HISTORICAL SOCIETY

Shootout electronic shooting gallery (located close to where the theater stood for over thirty years), the refreshment stand, a row of game booths including the fish pond game, and a fortune teller. Above the game booths on the right stands a wooded hill with picnic shelters.

After a few steps further north, a visitor reaches two of Idora's star attractions: the PTC #61 carousel, listed since 1975 on the National Register of Historic Places, and the Wildcat coaster, ranked in the top ten in the United States. Across from the Wildcat loading station is the Penny Arcade with its many machines and video games. Here one can play As-

A wheel game on the midway.
PHOTOGRAPH BY RICK SHALE

The Jack Rabbit was an out-and-back coaster.
PHOTOGRAPH BY CHARLES J. JACQUES, JR.

1981 - 1984

Idora Limited circled the picnic hill.
MICHAEL BROWN COLLECTION

The Cheyenne Shootout, an electronic shooting gallery.
MICHAEL BROWN COLLECTION

The Ferris Wheel was covered with lights.
PHOTOGRAPH BY RICK SHALE

Enjoying candy floss at a company picnic.
MICHAEL BROWN COLLECTION

teroids, Sky Raider, or Space Firebird; test one's skill at the Rifle Range, Road Test, or Slugger machines; or manipulate a claw crane to grab a favorite prize.

Beyond the Arcade the park broadens into the upper midway. To the right is the famous Idora French fries stand, and in the center of the midway is the Rocket Ship ride. Under the Rocket Ships is the Rocket Lunching Pad where one can buy cotton candy, hot dogs, waffles, or pizza. To the left is a refreshment stand where one can buy a hot dog on a stick and the game booth where one can play Idora (the familiar bingo game except the cards spell Idora instead of bingo).

In the northwest corner of the park stands the Crazy Horse Saloon, though old-timers would know it as Heidelberg Gardens. This is the oldest building in Idora, dating from 1899 when it was called the Casino and housed the park's first dancing pavilion. Situated in a row along the park's northern border are the Kooky Castle, a dark ride; Laffin' Lena's Loonyland, formerly known as the Whacky Shack and before that as simply the Fun House; and Helter Skelter, the modern version of the old Dodgem cars. Next to Helter Skelter is the northern entrance to the park from Parkview Avenue.

Kiddieland's hot rod cars were imported from Germany.
PHOTOGRAPH BY CHARLES J. JACQUES, JR.

Guarding the entrance to Kiddieland.
PHOTOGRAPH BY CHARLES J. JACQUES, JR.

Gypsy Grandma in the Penny Arcade.
EDWARD C. LEARNER COLLECTION

Riding the Pinto Fire Engine in Kiddieland.
MICHAEL BROWN COLLECTION

In front of Loonyland is the Scrambler and just east of the Rocket Ships are the Ferris Wheel, the Tilt-A-Whirl, and the Caterpillar. Nearby is the station for the Idora Limited with its C. P. Huntington train that circles the wooded hill and picnic shelters. Just east of the Ferris Wheel is the Paratrooper ride and a white stone house that contains a women's restroom.

Next to the Paratrooper is the entrance to Kiddieland, guarded by two Nutcracker soldiers. Idora's swimming pool was located where Kiddieland's fourteen rides now stand. From the entrance and walking clockwise, a visitor will find a Wet Boat ride, Pinto Fire Engine, Kiddie Coaster, Tubs of Fun, Skyfighter, Bulgey the Whale, Pinto Pony Cart, Mangels Kiddie Whip, Kiddie Turtle, Jet Swing, Hobby Horse ride, Hampton Dry Boats, Hot Rods and a Mangels Kiddie Carousel. In the center of Kiddieland is a miniature train which circles a grass island dotted with three flower beds.

Outside of Kiddieland in the park's northeast corner where an outdoor roller skating rink once stood is the Hooterville Highway with its antique cars, and inside the track stands the Flying Scooter ride.

Despite a loss of revenue, Pat Duffy and the other owners were optimistic about the 1984 season. "I do see a light at

1981 - 1984

Lost River entrance.
PHOTOGRAPH BY PAUL KOROL

Lost River elephant.
MICHAEL BROWN COLLECTION

The Wildcat was one of America's best coasters.
PHOTOGRAPH BY RICHARD MUNCH

the end of the tunnel," Duffy told *Amusement Business* in December. But four months later on April 26, 1984, disaster struck, and that light at the end of the tunnel went dark.

A spark from an untended welder's torch ignited a fire on the Lost River ride. Brisk winds fanned the blaze, and the fire spread quickly to the Wildcat and park office. Nearly fifty firefighters battled the blaze for hours, many of them off-duty firemen who worked without compensation. The fire was finally put out, but the damage was extensive.

The south turn of the Wildcat was destroyed in the fire, as were the Lost River ride and eleven concession and game stands on the midway. The park

The midway in flames.
©The Vindicator, 1999

office was also destroyed and the Turtle badly damaged. But firefighters saved the carousel, and the ballroom and Jack Rabbit were untouched. No one was injured although several firefighters were treated for smoke inhalation. Red Cross personnel served refreshments to the firefighters and park employees who battled the blaze.

Pat Duffy feared that the cost to rebuild the Wildcat was prohibitive but vowed to open the park. He told the *Plain Dealer*, "As word of our disaster hit the news wires I got calls from park operators all over the country offering to send portable rides, concessions or anything else that would help us open our season on time next week."

Surveying the damage. L to R: Pat Duffy, Jr.; park secretary Linda Loparo; Leonard Cavalier; Max Rindin.
© The Vindicator, 1999

The midway in ruins.
Photograph by Rick Shale

117

1981 - 1984

Youngstowners came to view the fire damage.
PHOTOGRAPH BY CHARLES J. JACQUES, JR.

Portable trailers were brought in after the fire.
© THE VINDICATOR, 1999

Host Larry Walk and his assistant Lydia watch Marion Lush at a 1984 Idora polka festival.
LARRY WALK COLLECTION

In spite of the fire Idora opened the 1984 season on schedule on May 5th, and a crowd of three to four thousand braved rainy weather to attend the WHOT Spring Thing. Portable trailers lined the midway replacing the permanent structures that had been destroyed.

The fire had not damaged the ballroom, and it was fully booked for the summer. Polka stars Frankie Yankovic and Walt Ostanek headlined the Spring Slovenfest, and Marion Lush, Wanda and Stephanie, Li'l Wally, and Eddie Blazonczyk's Versatones came to Idora for the Penn-Ohio Polka Festival in June.

The park's remaining coaster offered a new look. Plans had been made even before the fire to run the cars of the Jack Rabbit backwards. The old coaster was renamed the Back Wabbit. Thirty of the thirty-two rides that had operated in 1983 were again in use, but the demise of the Wildcat and Lost River ride had a negative effect on attendance. The loss of these attractions also meant fewer employees were needed; about 210 workers were hired in 1984, down from the usual 250.

Following the fire a rumor started that the park was closed. Even increased advertising and cooperation from the news media could not stop the rumors. Attendance dropped about 35 percent. Finally, the inevitable had to be faced. "We'd operated in the red the last two seasons," confessed Duffy. "We were going downhill fast."

On August 28th, with the charred remains of the Wildcat as a backdrop, the three park owners Pat Duffy, Jr., Max Rindin, and Leonard Cavalier announced that Idora would close for good after the Labor Day weekend. "With new rides ranging in price from $50,000 for a kiddie ride to more than $500,000 for a major ride, we are simply prohibited from competing with the major national theme parks." Duffy explained. The headlines that night read: "Idora Park Will Fold; Ballroom May Remain."

Fittingly for a park that netted over half of its annual revenue from company picnics, the final time Idora Park operated as an amusement park was for a company picnic. On Saturday, September 8th, employees of St. Elizabeth's Hospital gathered to take the last rides in Idora's history.

The Jack Rabbit became the Back Wabbit in the park's final season.
PHOTOGRAPH BY CHARLES J. JACQUES, JR.

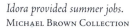

Idora provided summer jobs.
MICHAEL BROWN COLLECTION

The Crazy Horse Saloon, formerly Heidelberg Gardens.
PHOTOGRAPH BY CHARLES J. JACQUES, JR.

Swinging at Idora.
MICHAEL BROWN COLLECTION

1981 - 1984

Auctioning off the midway prizes.
©The Vindicator, 1999

(Right) Waiting for a buyer.
© The Vindicator, 1999

Auction crowd at Loonyland.
Photograph by Charles J. Jacques, Jr.

Since Duffy, Cavalier, and Rindin had not been able to find a buyer, they contracted with an auctioneer to sell the rides and equipment. The auction on October 20-21, 1984, was conducted by Norton Auctioneers of Coldwater, Michigan. A crowd of about eight hundred attended. All rides, concessions, games, and equipment were auctioned off: the hot dog grills and root beer barrels; the machines for making snow cones, cotton candy, and funnel cakes; the fryers that made those wonderful Idora French fries; the park benches and picnic tables; the old street lights and the new laser games from the Arcade all were sold. Everything from the memorable to the mundane went under the auctioneer's hammer. "Ho, ho! You're off the money," the auctioneer shouted when some bids fell below his expectations.

Many of the rides were sold to other park operators who had traveled to Idora to see what bargains they could pick up. On the big rides the auction crew in red blazers and sunglasses scanned the crowd for bidders like secret service agents searching for assassins. Some of the bids were surprising. The Spider went for $61,000, but the Ferris Wheel brought a surprisingly low bid of only $2,500. The C. P. Huntington train was sold for $28,500. "Where are you going to buy another one today?" said the auctioneer as he searched the audience for any last bids.

The most dramatic moment at the auction was the sale of the park's historic carousel. In the weeks leading up to the auction, a feverish campaign to save the carousel had been waged with local politicians including Mayor Pat Ungaro attempting to keep the ride intact and in the Youngstown area. These plans, however, fell through, and on October 20th the merry-go-round went on the block. The fear was that this historic Philadelphia Toboggan Company carousel #61 would be broken up and sold to individual collectors and dealers.

Auctioneer David Norton explained that he would first take bids on the individual horses. Then he would auction off the rounding boards and mechanical devices. These bids would be totaled and 10 percent would be added. Bidding would then be reopened for the entire carousel.

Bidding on the individual hand-carved, wooden horses was brisk, and the opening bid on the lead horse was $10,000. "Yes, ma'am," said the auctioneer to an astonished woman in the crowd. "That was $10,000. This is no place for sightseers." Bids on the outside row of horses averaged $11,500, and one armored horse brought a bid of $23,500. After bidding on the individual horses concluded and the amounts were totaled,

Tagged for sale.
© THE VINDICATOR, 1999

Buyers bid on the Kiddieland train.
PHOTOGRAPH BY CHARLES J. JACQUES, JR.

1981 - 1984

The Wildcat loading station after the park closed.
PHOTOGRAPH BY CHARLES J. JACQUES, JR.

An abrupt end to the Wildcat.
PHOTOGRAPH BY RICK SHALE

The deserted carousel pavilion.
PHOTOGRAPH BY CHARLES J. JACQUES, JR.

the auctioneer announced that it would take an offer of at least $385,000 to buy the carousel as a unit. "Who'll give half a million dollars for it?" he asked. "Who'll give half a million, where?" The crowd remained silent. "Give me $385,000 or it will sell individually. $385,000, where?" Then a mighty roar from the crowd erupted as David and Jane Walentas, a couple from New York City, signaled they would meet that price. No other bids were forthcoming, and the gavel fell. The Idora carousel would remain intact.

No official figures were released, but the auction was thought to have brought in about $700,000, about half the asking price for the entire park. Neither the Wildcat nor the Jack Rabbit was sold, though their cars were auctioned off. The ballroom remained and was booked with attractions through the spring.

Sadly, only ten weeks after the auction Pat Duffy Jr. died of a heart attack. He was fifty-seven years old and had worked at Idora since he was nine when his father put him to work selling grab bags. His father had started at the park in 1905, and his two sons also worked at Idora. Pat Duffy III was games superintendent, and Mike Duffy was rides superintendent. A *Vindicator* editorial noted that Pat Duffy, Jr. "won the respect and affection of all who knew him personally." George Nelson, a former Idora employee, wrote in the Youngstown State University *Jambar*: "Some have said they felt Mr. Duffy's death was foreshadowed by the end of Idora. I don't know about that. I do know that Mr. Duffy died after devoting a lifetime to making people happy. Other people have died with a lot less to be said for them."

Weeds replaced rides in Kiddieland.
PHOTOGRAPH BY CHARLES J. JACQUES, JR.

Goodbye, Idora.
PHOTOGRAPH BY RICK SHALE

POSTSCRIPT

Fifteen years have passed since Idora Park closed, and not much remains. Shortly after the auction all rides except the roller coasters were removed. A fire in 1986 wiped out the corner of the park where the Crazy Horse Saloon, Kooky Castle, Laffin' Lena's Loonyland, and the Helter Skelter building once stood. The carousel building and the penny arcade have been demolished, and the midway is now weed-choked and silent. The paint is peeling and the wood is rotting on the old bathhouse and the few remaining refreshment stands, and the ballroom is deteriorating badly. The scene is one of decay and abandonment.

Rather than mourn the demise of the park, however, we should celebrate the fact that Idora lasted as long as it did, longer by far than all but a few of the trolley parks that sprang up a century ago. The park may be gone, but the memories of the people who visited Idora live on.

MICHAEL BROWN COLLECTION

MICHAEL BROWN COLLECTION

Michael Brown Collection

Michael Brown Collection

St. Elizabeth Hospital Medical Center provided by Edward C. Learner

Edward C. Learner Collection

Michael Brown Collection

In our mind we can remember the warmth of a summer evening at Idora, a first visit to Kiddieland, or a slow ride on the Idora Limited as it looped through the park. We can still dance to "the sweetest music this side of heaven" in the ballroom or rock to Mike Roncone's band at the Kove South. We can still eat a hot dog on a stick or greasy Idora French fries from a paper cone and sip a cold beer in Heidelberg Gardens or a lemon shake on the midway.

We can still recall the darkness of the Kooky Castle, the winding tunnel of the Rapids, or when the cover of the Caterpillar came over us and can still hear the sounds of Idora: shouts of happy children in Kiddieland, music from the carousel's band organ, screams from the Wildcat, and the moronic laughter of the mechanical Fun House lady.

MICHAEL BROWN COLLECTION

MICHAEL BROWN COLLECTION

CHARLES J. JACQUES, JR. COLLECTION

Michael Brown Collection

Michael Brown Collection

Michael Brown Collection

Photograph by Marge Wood

Photograph by Betty Jacques

Our days at Idora Park were full of fun: watching the monkeys, riding a pony, trying to get through the revolving barrel in the Fun House, or winning a prize on the midway. Idora was where we shared a picnic lunch with family or friends in one of the park's shaded groves; where we felt the rush of the Wildcat's first drop and its bone-jarring turns or the graceful revolutions of the Rocket Ships; where we watched fireworks explode in the night sky.

These experiences will live forever, if only in our minds—where the last ride of summer never ends.

Photograph by Richard Munch

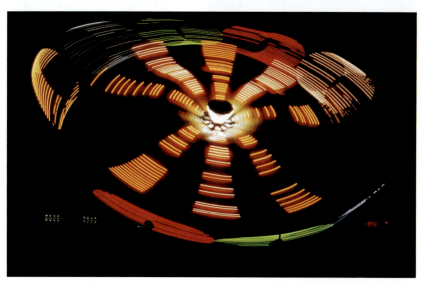

Photograph by Rick Shale

APPENDICES

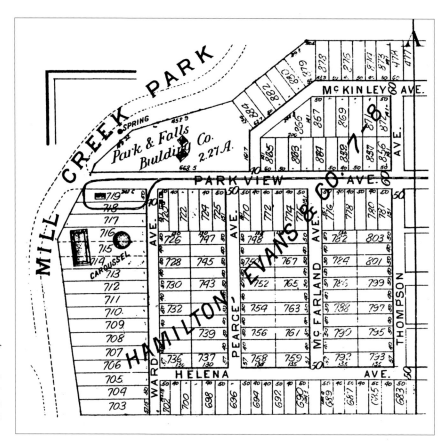

Terminal Park 1899

This map from the *Atlas of Surveys of Mahoning County, Ohio*, shows the route of the streetcar line on Parkview Avenue and a few buildings to be erected for the park's initial season.

Dance Orchestras

1910	Idora Park opens a new, ornate dance pavilion at the south end of the park. Boyle's Orchestra, which had already played at Idora for several seasons, is retained as the house orchestra.
1911	Boyle's Orchestra
1912	Boyle's Orchestra
1913	Boyle's Orchestra
1914	Boyle's Orchestra
1915	Boyle's Orchestra
1916	Boyle's Orchestra
1917	Boyle's Orchestra
1918	Boyle's Orchestra
1919	Boyle's Orchestra
1920	Boyle's Orchestra
1921	Ben Shulansky – Shulansky's Symphonic Syncopators
1922	Verne Ricketts and the Premier Orchestra of Chicago
1923	Verne Ricketts Orchestra
1924	Verne Ricketts Orchestra
1925	Bill Foley's Original Keystone Serenaders; Jimmy Dimmick's Sunnybrook Orchestra (after July 6th)
1926	Jimmy Dimmick's Sunnybrook Orchestra
1927	Jimmy Dimmick's Sunnybrook Orchestra
1928	Hy Steed and His Commodores
1929	Ace Brigode Orchestra
1930	Ace Brigode Orchestra
1931	Chic Scoggins Orchestra
1932	Freddie Bergin Orchestra
1933	Idora shifts from a tradition of booking a house orchestra for the season to a policy of booking name bands for shorter periods.

Ownership of the Property

1894-1911:	Lemuel T. Foster and Susanna B. Foster
1911-1923:	Willis H. Park
1923-1924:	J. F. Ritter and Harriet W. Ritter
1924:	Penn-Ohio Power & Light Company
1924-1949:	Idora Amusement Company
1949-1985:	Idora Amusement Company and Pat Duffy
1985-1987:	Mount Calvary Pentecostal Church
1987-1989:	Pro-Tem Management
1989-1994:	Consumers United Insurance Company
1994-Present:	Mount Calvary Pentecostal Church

Managers of Idora Park

1899-1904:	Ed Stanley
1905:	Col. J. H. Dietrick
1906:	Ed Kane
1907:	Bob Cunningham
1908-1909:	George Rose
1910:	Perry Barge
1911-1920:	Royal Platt
1921-1930:	Rex Billings
1931-1940:	Charlie Deibel
1941-1975:	Max Rindin
1975-1984:	Pat Duffy, Jr.

Selected List of Bands, Orchestras, and Vocal Artists That Played in the Idora Park Ballroom, 1910-1984

BANDS AND ORCHESTRAS:

Ray Anthony
Louis Armstrong
Artie Arnell
Eddie Arnel
Nick Bari (a.k.a. Nick Barile)
Nick Barile (a.k.a. Nick Bari)
Charlie Barnet
Lee Barrett
Gene Beecher
Freddie Bergin
Ben Bernie
Hank Biagini
Barry Blue
J. E. Boyle
Ace Brigode and His Fourteen Virginians
Ralph Britt
Les Brown
Dave Brubeck
Rudy Bundy
Paul Burton
Cab Calloway and his Cotton Club Orchestra
Joe Cann
Russ Carlyle
Tommy Carlyn
Bob Chester
Chicago Symphony
Tommy Christian
Johnny Cimino
Eddie Conti
Criss Cross
Warren Covington
Xavier Cugat
Chuck Curtis
Hal Curtis
Red Curtis
Bobby Dale
Paul Dale
Dolly Dawn and the Dawn Patrol
Jack Denny
Jimmy Dimmick's Sunnybrook Orchestra
Sam Donahue
Jimmy Dorsey
Tommy Dorsey
George Duffy
The Dukes of Dixieland
Larry Elgart
Les Elgart
Larry Faith
Art Farrar
Maynard Ferguson
Jerry Fielding
Ralph Flannigan
Myron Floren
Bill Foley's Original Keystone Serenaders
Larry Fotine Orchestra with Kitty Kallen
Frank Gallo
Jan Garber
Jimmie Garrigan
Emerson Gill
Wally Gingers
Don Glasser
Cecil Golly
Benny Goodman
Larry Green
Jon Greer
Jimmy Gunter
Ross Halamay
George Hall and the Hotel Taft Orchestra
Jess Hawkins
Richard Hayman
Noah Henderson
Woody Herman
Tiny Hill
Herbie Holmes
Eddie Howard
Pappy Howard
Dean Hudson
Brad Hunt
Pee Wee Hunt
Harry James
Benny Jones
Bobby Jones
Maurie Kates
Al Kavelin and his Cascading Chords Orchestra
Sammy Kaye
Lee Kelton
Stan Kenton
Wayne King
Angelo LaCivita
Buddy Lee
Jack Lewis
Guy Lombardo
Victor Lombardo
Carl Lorch
Ralph Marterie
Eddie Martin
Billy Maxted
Billy May
Clyde McCoy
Johnny McGee
Hal McIntire
Glenn Miller Orchestra (under the direction of Buddy DeFranco)
Glenn Miller Orchestra (under the direction of Jimmy Henderson)
Glenn Miller Orchestra (under the direction of Ray McKinley)
Vaughn Monroe
Russ Morgan
Buddy Morrow
Jimmy Muliadore
Johnny Murphy
Harold Nelson
Phil Nelson
Red Nichols and His Pennies Orchestra
Frank Orosz
Peter Palmer
Ray Pearl and his Sunset Orchestra
Teddy Phillips
Al Pierson
Col. Manny Prager and His Cavaliers
Alvino Ray
Buddy Rich
Verne Ricketts' Rythmonic Orchestra (1924)
Verne Ricketts and His Broadway Orchestra
Ray Robbins
Russ Romero
Mike Roncone
Glenn Ross
Sauter-Finegan Orchestra
Chic Scoggins
Artie Shaw
Shulansky's Symphonic Syncopators
Lou Sikora
Arlie Simmonds
Del Sinchak
Noble Sissle
Dick Stabile
Stan Stanley
Hy Steed and His Commodores
Ted Stults and His Carnegie Tartans
Theodore Thomas
Tommy Tucker
Bob Vinton
George Wald
Bill Warner
Ted Weems
Lawrence Welk
Zack Whyte and his Twelve Chocolate Beau Brummels
Hod Williams
Kai Winding
Billy Yates and his Orchestra
Youngstown Military Band
Youngstown Symphony
Si Zentner

POLKA:

Jim Ament
Ampoltones
Ampolaires
Tom Balicky's Harmony Tones
Bill Basilone
Bill Bevec
Big Steve and Buffalo Bel-Aires
Eddie Blazonczyk and the Versatones
Brass Connection
Ray Budzilek
Johnny Butchko
Canadian Fiddlestix
Casinos
John Detelich
Dynasonics
Dynasounds
Dynatones
Eddie and the Slovenes
Joe Fedor and the Polish All Stars
Joe Fedorchak
Golden Brass
Stas Golonka and His Chicago Masters
Lenny Gomulka and Chicago Push
Goral Boys
Pat Gray
Ed Guca's Polish Canadians
Hank Haller
Happy Louie
Happy Richie
Happy Tony and the Coal Diggers
Harmony Sharps
Henni and Versa J's
Holy Toledo
John Hyzny
Invictas
Ray Jay and Carousels
Jolly J's
Jumping Jacks
Frank Kalik
King Brothers
Johnny Krizancic
Koslosky's Rhythm-Airs
Li'l Richard
Li'l Wally
Marion Lush and the White Eagles
Joe Luzar
Eddie Mack
Maddie's Polish Princes
Mahoning Valley Button Box
Melody Kings
Jimmy Mieszala and Music Explosion
Bruno Mikos and Harmony Stars
Joey Miskulin
Al Nowak
Joe Oberaitis and His Musical Sharps
Walt Ostanek
Pala Brothers
Pan Juzef
Johnny Pecon
Penn-Ohio Button Box
John Plescha's Del-Fi's
Polish Canadians
Polish Friends
Polka Jets
Polka Stars
Roman Possedi
Eddie Potoniec
Sam Pugliano
Ranata and Girls, Girls, Girls
Raytones
Syl Rutkowski
Del Sinchak
Sounds
Spectacular Polka Aires
Stanky and the Coal Miners
Steel City Brass
Alvin Styczynski
Sunshine
Jack Tady
Jerry Tarka and Mid-West Sounds
John Tasz
The Tick-Tockers
Bobby Timko
Toledo Polkamotion
Toledo Troubadours
Treltones
Richie Vadnal
Verna's Polish Highlanders
Wally's Polka Chips
Wanda and Stephanie
Matt Wasielewski and the Polka Jets
Windy City Brass
Frank Wojnarowski
Frankie Yankovic
Markic- Zagger

ROCK AND ROLL, COUNTRY, POP OR VOCAL ARTISTS:

Bay City Rollers
Blue Oyster Cult
James Brown
The Byrds
David Cassidy
Roy Clark
Commander Cody and the Lost Planet Airmen
Billy "Crash" Craddock
Danny and the Juniors
The DeFranco Family
Joe Dowell
The Eagles
El Dorados
Every Mother's Son
The Four Aces
Four Freshmen
The Gaylords
Gerry Granahan
Human Beingz
K. C. and the Sunshine Band
The Limelighters
Looking Glass
The Mersey Men
The Monkees
Ohio Express
Poni-Tails
The Raspberries
Jody Reynolds
Bobby Rydell
Sam the Sham and the Pharaohs
Bobby Sherman
Michael Stanley Band
Conway Twitty
Jackie Wilson

Professional Baseball Teams That Played At Idora Park

Major Leagues:
Boston Red Sox
Brooklyn Dodgers
Cincinnati Reds
Cleveland Indians
New York Giants
Philadelphia Phillies
Pittsburgh Pirates
St. Louis Browns

Negro Leagues:
Birmingham Black Barons
Chicago American Giants
Cleveland Buckeyes
Cleveland Tate Stars
Homestead Grays
Kansas City Monarchs
Newark Eagles
New York Cubans
Philadelphia Stars

Other:
Bloomer Girls
House of David
King and His Court

Idora Park Rides and Attractions Offered For Sale at the Auction, October 20-21, 1984

Major Rides:
Rock-O-Plane
Spider
C.P. Huntington Train
Paratrooper
Scrambler
Turtle
Ferris Wheel
Tilt-A-Whirl
Rocket Ride
Helter Skelter (12 Spaggiari Duce dodge-em cars)
Caterpillar
Wildcat Roller Coaster (not operating)
Jack Rabbit Roller Coaster
Flying Scooters
Kooky Castle (dark ride)
1922 Carousel by Philadelphia Toboggan Company (#61)
Arrow Antique Autos

Kiddie Rides:
Bulgey the Whale
Pinto Fire Engine
Hampton Tubs of Fun
Pinto Pony Cart
Mangels Kiddie Whip
Allan Herschell Skyfighter
Turtle
Hobby Horse Merry-Go-Round
Mangels Kiddie Carousel
Allan Herschell Wet Boat Ride
Hampton Dry Boat Ride
Jet Swing
Junior Roller Coaster
Hot Rod Cars
Miniature Train

Members of Baseball's Hall of Fame at Cooperstown who played or appeared at Idora Park

Played in a game at the Idora ball field:
Walter Alston (Portsmouth and later Springfield in the Middle Atlantic League; inducted as manager)
Earl Averill (Cleveland Indians)
Dave Bancroft (New York Giants)
Oscar Charleston (Homestead Grays)
Ray Dandridge (Newark Eagles)
Leon Day (Newark Eagles)
Johnny Evers (New York Giants; was working as a player/coach when Giants visited Idora)
Frank Frisch (New York Giants)
Lefty Grove (1926 American League All-Star team; played for Philadelphia A's)
Judy Johnson (Homestead Grays)
George Kelly (New York Giants)
Buck Leonard (Homestead Grays)
Heinie Manush (1926 American League All-Star team; played for Detroit Tigers)
Bill McKechnie (Pittsburgh Pirates; inducted as manager)
Edd Roush (Cincinnati Reds)
Honus Wagner (Carnegie Elks; player-manager after career with Pittsburgh Pirates)
Willie Wells (Newark Eagles)
Ross Youngs (New York Giants)

Appeared but did not play:
Billy Evans (inducted as umpire-executive)
Rube Foster (manager of Chicago American Giants)
John McGraw (inducted as manager)
Cy Young (special guest appearance at a Middle Atlantic League game May 5, 1951)

Ride Capacity Per Hour

Adult Rides:	
Wildcat	1,050
Yo-Yo	800
Whacky Shack	750
Scrambler	650
Lost River	450
Caterpillar	600
Tilt-A-Whirl	550
Rockets	300
Carousel	600
Jack Rabbit	850
Spider	650
Hooterville Highway	400
Turtle	750
Train Ride	700
Flying Cages	175
Sky Wheel	250
Kooky Castle	400
Turbo	450
Paratrooper	400
Helter Skelter	850

Kiddie Land:	
Sky Fighter	200
Little Train	200
Hobby Horse	200
Coaster	350
Plane	200
Whip	200
Buggy	200
Kiddie Turtle	250
Gondola-Wet	250
Boats-Dry	250
Little Fire Engine	250
Tubs-O-Fun	250
Junior Hot Rods	350
Merry-Go-Round	200
Total:	**14,975**

Nationality Days at Idora Park

A partial listing of nationalities and related lodges or organizations that sponsored days at Idora Park to celebrate their ethnic and cultural heritage:

B'nai B'rith	Polish National Alliance
British Empire	Polish Societies
Croatian	Roumanian
Croatian Catholic	Roumanian Legion
German	Russian
German-American Central Society	St. David's Society
	Scotch
German Saxon Association	Scottish Clans
Greek	Serbian
Hungarian	Slovak
Independent Sons of Italy	Sokol
Irish	Sons of Italy
Italian	Swedish
Jewish	Ukrainian
National Polish Societies	United Irish Societies
National Slovenic Society	Welsh
Neapolitan Societies	Welsh Pioneers
Polish	Yugoslav

Idora Park Admission Prices

For much of its history, Idora Park did not charge an admission fee. Visitors came to the park at no charge and bought tickets to individual rides.

In 1967 the park began experimenting with a Pay-One-Price policy that included park admission and unlimited admission to all rides. At first the P-O-P policy was used only for holidays and special occasions. In 1974 the policy was extended to daily admission, though individual ride tickets were still available.

Year	Price
1967	$2.50
1968	$3.00
1969	$3.00
1970	$3.50
1971	$3.50
1972	$4.00
1973	$4.00
1974	$4.00
1975	$4.00
1976	$4.00
1977	$4.75
1978	$4.75
1979	$5.50
1980	$5.50
1981	$5.95
1982	$6.95
1983	$6.95
1984	$6.95

Theatrical Companies at Idora Park

From the first season in 1899 through the summer of 1913, patrons came to the Idora Park Theater to see vaudeville acts rather than dramatic presentations. These variety acts, at least five to six per show, were changed regularly, so each week might bring new performers to the park. The shows were generally booked by Keith and Proctor in New York. Occasionally during these years a play might be substituted for the vaudeville bill. The Horne Stock Company, for example, presented a play at Idora in 1910. In 1914, however, Idora switched from vaudeville to a policy of presenting summer stock. These stock companies would be booked for the season and would perform a new play every week.

1914	The Morton Opera Company
1915	The Morton Opera Company
1916	The Morton Musical Comedy Company
1917	The Horne Stock Company
1918	The Horne Stock Company
1919	The Horne Stock Company
1920	The Horne Stock Company
1921	The Horne Stock Company
1922	The James Burtis Players
1923	The Burns-Kasper Players
1924	The Lillian Desmonde Players
1925	The Lillian Desmonde Players
1926	The Lillian Desmonde Players
1927	The Lillian Desmonde Players
1928	The Lillian Desmonde Players
1929	The Tarona Players
1930	The Lillian Desmonde Players
1931	The Carlton Brickert Players, The Mary-Jane Lane Stock Company

By 1930 summer stock had begun to fade from the entertainment scene. The introduction of sound to motion pictures and shifts in public taste had their effect. Lillian Desmonde's husband and partner Jack Hammond died in 1930, and she disbanded her stock company. The Carlton Brickert Players were booked for 1931, but even featured stars such as Francis X. Bushman, who headlined the first production, could not sustain a full season of theater. Idora ended its policy of booking a stock company for the whole season, though plays continued to be presented. In 1932, for example, the Youngstown Players, a group of actors from the Youngstown Playhouse, performed at Idora. By the mid-1930s the theater was no longer used and after a few years was torn down.

Picnics at Idora Park

A partial listing of companies, schools, communities, lodges, and other organizations that booked picnics at Idora Park:

Akron Steelworkers
Aliquippa Sunday Schools
Alliance Machine Company
Alliance Review
Amalgamated Iron & Steel Workers
American Legion
American Legion Drum Corps
American Legion Post 472, Road of Remembrance
American Steel Foundry
American Welding Company of Warren, OH
Armco Steel
Armstrong Cork of Pittsburgh
Atwater Township Schools
Austintown Community Family Fun Day
Austintown Schools
Aut Mori Grotto
Babcock & Wilcox Tube Company of Beaver Falls, PA
B & W Tube Company of Alliance
Beaver County Schools
Beaver Falls Schools
Beaver Public Schools
Beaver Valley Industrial Picnic Association
Bixler's Kiddie Day
Black and Decker
Blackhawk Schools
Brookfield Schools
Butler County Merchants
Campbell Schools
Carnegie Steel Company
Catholic Knights of St. George of Pittsburgh
Center Township Schools
Cities Service Company of Warren
C.M.B.A. of Northern Ohio
Colored Day
Colored Elks
Colored Masons of Pittsburgh
Columbiana County Schools
Columbiana Day
Columbiana Foundry
Commercial Printing Company of Akron
Copperweld Steel
Crucible Steel
Deaf Mute Convention and Outing
Deming Pump Company of Salem
Diebold
East Liverpool Schools
Erie Railroad Veterans' Association
E. W. Bliss Company of Salem
Firestone Tire and Rubber Company
First Catholic Slovak Ladies Union
Fitch High School
Foresters of America of Eastern Ohio
Fraternal Order of Eagles
Free and Accepted Masons, Covenant Lodge #59
Friendly Writers' Club
General American Activities Association
General Dry Battery Company of Cleveland
General Fireproofing Company
General Motors–Lordstown
G. M. McKelvey Company
Goodrich Tires
Goodyear Rubber
Gougler Machine

Groundhog Lodges of Cleveland and Youngstown
Hebron Lodge
H. H. Robertson
Holland Bread Kiddie Day
Hoover Sweeper Company of Canton
Hopewell Schools
Horse Shoers of Pennsylvania and Ohio
Hubbard P.T.A. Family Day
Independent Order of Odd Fellows
International Steel Equipment Company
Isaly Day
Italian-American Political Association
Johnson Bronze Company
Junior Labor Day
Junior Saxons Day
Knights of St. George of Pittsburgh
Knights of the Golden Eagle of Eastern Ohio and Western PA
Koppers Company of Kobuta, PA
Ku Klux Klan
Lamson-Sessions
Lawrence County Schools
Lutheran Day
Maccabees of Akron
Mahoning County Schools
Mahoning County Sunday School Association
Mahoning County Teachers
Mahoning Valley Council Boy Scouts
Mahoning Valley Hospital
Mahoning Valley Industrial Management
Masonic Day
Mercer County Schools
Midland Schools
Milliken Kiddie Day
Monaca Public Schools
Morgan Engineering
Motorcycle Dealers and Clubs
Mullins Manufacturing Company of Warren, OH
National Defense Day
New Brighton Area Schools and Community
New Brighton Teachers Alumnae
New Castle Schools
Niles Rolling Mill
Northwestern Beaver Schools
Ohio Edison (Youngstown, Warren, Alliance)
Ohio Public Service of Warren
Packard Electric
Parochial Schools
Peerless Electric
P.H.C. of Oil City, Franklin, and Meadville, PA
Pittsburgh & Lake Erie Railroad
Pittsburgh & Lake Erie Railroad Shop Men
Pittsburgh Order of Independent Americans
Potters Picnic
P.T.A. School Day
Pyramid Rubber Company
Republic Rubber Company
Republic Steel
Rochester Schools
Roumanian Legion Outing
St. Casimir's School
St. Elizabeth Hospital

St. Joseph Lead Company
St. Stanislaus School
Sanitary Milk Company
Schwebel Bread Company
Scottish Rite
Scout Day
Seiberling Tire and Rubber Company
Shenango Pottery Company of New Castle
South Side Civics Association
South Side Day
Southside Merchants Day
Spang-Chalfant Company of Ambridge, PA
Springfield Township Schools
Steelworkers Day
Stevens Metal Manufacturing Company
Strong Enamel Company
Strong Manufacturing Company
Strouss–Hirshberg Company
Struthers Day
Struthers Schools
Sunlight Electric Company
Tabernacle Baptist Church
Teamsters
Thomas Steel Company
Tri-County Farmers Grange
Trumbull County Schools
Truscon Steel Company
T.R.W.
Twin Coach
Union Township Schools
United Brick and Clay Workers of America
United Brotherhood of Lutheran Churches
United Engineering Company of New Castle
United Engineering Company of Youngstown
United Steelworkers of America Local 1190
Vasa Association of America
Villa Maria Home
Vindicator Carriers and Salesmen
Vindicator High School Play Day
Vindicator Kiddie Day
Warren Retail Grocers' Association
Wean
Western Beaver Schools
Westinghouse Electric Company of Monaca, PA
West Side Business Men's Outing
West Side Day
WFMJ Day
WHOT Day
WNIO Day
WYTV Day
Y.M.H.A.
Youngstown Hospitals
Youngstown Letter Carriers
Youngstown Parent-Teacher Association
Youngstown Retail Grocers and Meat Dealers Association
Youngstown Sheet and Tube Company
Youngstown Silent Club
Youngstown State University Day (IFC/Pan Hellenic)

A Selected List of Amusement Parks and Resorts Located Within 125 Miles of Idora Park, Youngstown, Ohio

Avon Park, Girard, OH *(formerly Squaw Creek Park and Ferncliffe Park)*
Beerside Park, Akron, OH
Blue Pond Park, Akron, OH
Cascade Park, New Castle, PA
Cedar Point, Sandusky, OH
Chippewa Lake Park, near Medina, OH
Conneaut Lake Park, Conneaut, PA
Craig Beach Park, near Diamond, OH
Euclid Beach Park, Cleveland, OH
Exposition Park, Conneaut, PA *(became Conneaut Lake Park)*
Ferncliffe Park, Girard, OH *(became Avon Park)*
Geauga Lake Park, Aurora, OH
High Bridge Glens Park, (Gorge Park), Akron, OH
Idlewild Park, Ligonier, PA
Kelly Park, Leetonia, OH
Kennywood Park, West Mifflin, PA
Lake Brady Park, near Akron, OH *(between Kent and Ravenna)*
Lake Park, Alliance, OH
Lakeside Park, Akron, OH *(became Summit Beach Park)*
Lakeside Park, Stoneboro, PA
Lake View Park, Canton, OH *(became Meyers Lake Park)*
Luna Park, Cleveland, OH
Luna Park, Pittsburgh, PA
Maple Beech Park, Alliance, OH
Meyers Lake Park, Canton, OH *(originally Lake View Park)*
Minerva Park, Minerva, OH
Monarch Park, Oil City, PA
Orchard Lake Park, Hudson, OH
Playland Park, near Akron, OH
Puritas Springs Park, Cleveland, OH
Randolph Park, Akron, OH
Riverside Park, near Akron, OH
Rock Springs Park, Chester, WV
Springfield Lake Park, near Akron, OH
Squaw Creek Park, Girard, OH *(became Ferncliffe Park and then Avon Park)*
Stanton Park, Steubenville, OH
Summit Beach Park, Akron, OH *(originally Lakeside Park)*
Sunnyside Park, Akron, OH
Terrapin Park, Parkersburg, WV
Tuscora Park, New Philadelphia, OH
Waldameer Park, Erie, PA
West View Park, Pittsburgh, PA
Wheeling Park, Wheeling, WV
White City Park, Cleveland, OH
White Swan Park, Pittsburgh, PA
Woodland Beach Park, Ashtabula, OH

On May 3, 1986, fire destroyed the buildings that once housed Heidelberg Gardens, Kooky Castle, Laffin' Lena's Loonyland, and Helter Skelter.
© THE VINDICATOR 1999

After the End: Idora Since 1985

In October 1985 Mount Calvary Pentecostal Church of Youngstown purchased Idora Park, and Rev. Norman L. Wagner announced plans for the construction of a $50 million religious community. This "City of God" would include a new church building, a seven-story prayer tower, a small shopping center, nursing home, private residences, and educational buildings. Construction was scheduled to begin in the spring of 1987.

On May 3, 1986, after the property had lain dormant for a year and a half, Idora was hit with another fire. This time the fire destroyed the northwest corner of the park. Among the buildings destroyed were the Kooky Castle, Laffin' Lena's Loonyland, the Helter Skelter bumper car ride, and the Crazy Horse Saloon. All rides and equipment of value had been removed from the park after the auction, but the fire still represented a historic loss. Heidelberg Gardens, recently re-themed as the Crazy Horse Saloon, was the oldest building on the property, dating from the park's first season in 1899.

May 1986 also marked the closure of the Idora Park ballroom. Several events had been booked prior to the sale of the property to the church, and May marked the end of those advanced bookings. Among the final events were the East Side Kiwanis Club annual spring dance, the Boardman High School prom, and a testimonial dinner for Clingan Jackson, retiring as the *Vindicator's* political writer. Mount Calvary Pentecostal Church announced it would take no further bookings, and the ballroom, after 77 seasons, closed its doors for good after May 25th.

In the next two and a half years, no activity occurred at Idora. The weeds grew, and the former park fell into a state of abandonment and disrepair as the buildings and coasters slowly faded and rotted. Mount Calvary was unable to come up with sufficient capital to put into action the plans for its "City of God."

On October 7, 1988, almost three years after the church had purchased the property, Mahoning County Common Pleas Judge Charles J. Bannon signed a foreclosure judgment against Mount Calvary. The church owed approximately half a million dollars to its creditors, including $250,000 to Consumers United Insurance Company of Washington, D. C., which held the mortgage.

After six months of negotiation and attempts to raise money, the church ran out of time. On May 2, 1989, a sheriff's auction was held, and Consumers United Insurance Company, the mortgage holder, bought the Idora property for $205,000 to protect its investment. The property was immediately put up for sale with local realtor Fred D'Amico acting as broker.

The failure to find any buyer and the increasing deterioration of the property prompted the formation of two preservation groups in the early 1990s. The Mahoning Valley Preservation Club was formed in 1991 to explore ways of revitalizing the Idora ballroom. The following year a number of members split off to form the Idora Park Historical Society. The new group succeeded in placing Idora Park on the National Register of Historic Places, but acrimonious disagreements among the group's officers ultimately led to the disbanding of the society. One former officer, Richard Scarsella, formed the Idora Park Institute and has continued the lobbying efforts to preserve at least some part of the park.

In January 1994 Mount Calvary Pentecostal Church repurchased Idora Park with a $300,000 loan from Teen Missions International of Florida. The church declared its intention to pursue the plan originally announced in 1987: to develop the property into a City of God. But in the next five years, no development occurred. The only activity has been demolition, not construction, and the property remains unused as the community celebrates the 100th anniversary of Idora Park's founding. The ballroom remains shuttered, and the Wildcat and Jack Rabbit roller coasters continue to deteriorate.

A sign on the Jack Rabbit currently advertises a future City of God.
PHOTOGRAPH BY RICK SHALE

The videotape *Idora Park* is available for purchase from Edward C. Learner, 2366 Wyandotte Ave., Cuyahoga Falls, OH 44223. Length: 72 minutes. Cost: $20.00 (includes shipping and handling). Ohio residents add $1.15 tax. Free ticket from Idora Park included with each tape.

Photographs in this book credited to Historic Images, as well as other Idora Park photographs and memorabilia, are available for purchase from Historic Images, 621 E. Main Street, Canfield, OH 44446. Contact Tom Molocea or Laurie Molocea at (330) 702-0702.

The Idora Park Institute is a non-profit study, advocacy, and historical group dedicated to the preservation of Idora's memory and the restoration of all or part of Idora Park. For information, contact founder and director Richard Scarsella at (330) 726-8277.

Those interested in additional reading about amusement parks may find the following periodicals and organizations helpful:

Amusement Business
Box 24970
Nashville, TN 37203

Amusement Today
P. O. Box 5427
Arlington, TX 76005-5427

At the Park
P. O. Box 597783
Chicago, IL 60659-7783

The Carousel News & Trader
87 Park Ave. West, Suite 206
Mansfield, OH 44902-1657

Merry-Go-Roundup
Publication of the National Carousel
  Association
P. O. Box 4333
Evansville, IN 47724-0333

NAPHA NEWS
Publication of the National Amusement
  Park Historical Association
P. O. Box 83
Prospect, IL 60056

Park World
P. O. Box 54
Desborough, Northants
England
NN14 2UH

RollerCoaster!
Publication of the American
  Coaster Enthusiasts
P. O. Box 8226
Chicago, IL 60680

SELECTED BIBLIOGRAPHY

Books:

Adams, Judith A. *The American Amusement Park Industry: A History of Technology and Thrills*. Boston: Twayne, 1991. 225 pp.; indexed with a bibliography.

Aley, Howard C. *A Heritage To Share: The Bicentennial History of Youngstown and Mahoning County, Ohio*. Youngstown, OH: Bicentennial Commission of Youngstown and Mahoning County, 1975. 589 pp; indexed with a bibliography.

Allegheny County Illustrated, 1896.
 Contains brief sketches of Robert McAfee, John R. Murphy, and Joseph Hastings, three of Idora's founders.

Atlas of Mahoning County, Ohio From Actual Surveys by and Under the Direction of D. J. Lake, C. E. Philadelphia: Titus, Simmons, & Titus, 1874.
 Labels the falls on Mill Creek as Idora Falls; the business directory lists Idora Mills half a mile west of Fosterville.

Atlas of Surveys of Mahoning County, Ohio. Philadelphia: A.H. Mueller Co., 1899-1900. Plate 15 shows the route of the Park & Falls line down Parkview Ave. A carousel building is also indicated.

Biographical History of Northeastern Ohio.
 Chicago: Lewis Publishing, 1893.
 Contains a lengthy profile of Col. Lemuel T. Foster on whose land Idora was built.

Blower, James M., and Robert Korach. *The N.O.T. & L. Story*. Chicago: Central Electric Railfans Association, 1966.

Blue, Fred, William D. Jenkins, H. William Lawson, and Joan M. Reedy. *Mahoning Memories: A History of Youngstown and Mahoning County*. Virginia Beach, VA: The Donning Company, 1995. 192 pp.; indexed with a bibliography.

Bush, Lee O., Edward C. Chukayne, Russell Allon Hehr, and Richard F. Hershey. *Euclid Beach Park Is Closed For the Season*. Mentor, OH: Amusement Park Books, 1977. 331 pp.; indexed with a bibliography.

Bush, Lee, and Richard F. Hershey. *Conneaut Lake Park: The First Hundred Years of Fun*. Fairview Park, OH: Amusement Park Books, 1992. 175 pp.; indexed with a bibliography.

Butler, Joseph G. *History of Youngstown and the Mahoning Valley, Ohio*. 3 vols. Chicago: American Historical Society, 1921.

Cartmell, Robert. *The Incredible Scream Machine: a History of the Roller Coaster*. Fairview Park, OH: Amusement Park Books, and Bowling Green, OH: Bowling Green State University Popular Press, 1987. 252 pp.; indexed with a bibliography.

Clark, Dick and Larry Lester, eds. *The Negro Leagues Book*. Cleveland: Society for American Baseball Research, 1994.

Electric Railways of Northeastern Ohio. Bulletin 108. Chicago: Central Electric Railfans Association, 1965. 223 pages.

Higley, George. *Youngstown: An Intimate History*. Youngstown, OH: n.p., 1953. 172 pp.

Hilton, George W. and John F. Due. *The Electric Interurban Railways in America*. Stanford: Stanford University Press, 1964. 463 pp.; index and with a bibliography. Includes information on the Mahoning & Shenango Railway and Light Company, Youngstown and Southern Railway, Youngstown and Ohio River Railroad, and many other transportation lines in Northeastern Ohio. The authors note, "No state approached within a thousand miles of Ohio's interurban mileage of 2,798."

Jacques, Charles J., Jr. *Goodbye, West View Park, Goodbye*. Natrona Heights, PA: Amusement Park Journal, 1985. 124 pp.; indexed with a bibliography.

_____. *Kennywood: Roller Coaster Capital of the World*. Vestal, NY: Vestal Press, 1982. 203 pp.; indexed.

_____. *More Kennywood Memories*. Jefferson, OH: Amusement Park Journal, 1998. 217 pp.; indexed.

Jenkins, William D. *Steel Valley Klan: The Ku Klux Klan in Ohio's Mahoning Valley*. Kent, OH: Kent State University Press, 1990. 222 pp.; indexed with a bibliography.

Jordan, John W., ed. *Encyclopedia of Pennsylvania Biography*. NY: Lewis Historical Publishing Co., 1916. Vol. 7 contains a sketch of Samuel Grier, one of Idora's founders.

Kyriazi, Gary. *The Great American Amusement Parks*. Secaucus, NJ: Citadel Press, 1976.

Martin, Carol. *Dance Marathons: Performing American Culture of the 1920s and 1930s*. Jackson, MS: University Press of Mississippi, 1994.

Munch, Richard. *Harry G. Traver: Legends of Terror*. Mentor, OH: Amusement Park Books, 1982. 174 pp.; indexed with a bibliography.

Nye, David. *Electrifying America: Social Meanings of a New Technology, 1880-1940*. Cambridge, MA: MIT Press, 1990. 479 pp.; indexed with a bibliography and extensive notes.

Obojski, Robert. *Bush League: A History of Minor League Baseball*. NY: Macmillan, 1975.

Paschen, Stephen H. *Shootin' the Chutes: Amusement Parks Remembered*. Akron, OH: Summit County Historical Society, 1988. 70 pp; indexed with a bibliography. A brief but useful survey of amusement parks in northeast Ohio with the primary focus on Summit County.

Rook, Charles, ed. *Western Pennsylvanians*. Pittsburgh: Biographical Association, 1923. Contains an entry on Charles W. Dahlinger, one of Idora's founders.

Rohrbeck, Benson W. *Notes From Pennsylvania's Street Railways*. West Chester, PA: Ben Rohrbeck Traction Publications, 1984.

Rowsome, Frank, Jr. *Trolley Car Treasury: A Century of American Streetcars—Horsecars, Cable Cars, Interurbans, and Trolleys*. NY: McGraw-Hill, 1956. 200 pp.; no index or bibliography. A very useful popular history of early public transportation; heavily illustrated.

Sanderson, General Thomas W. *Twentieth Century History of Youngstown and Mahoning County, Ohio and Its Representative Citizens*. Chicago: Biographical Publishing Co., 1907.

Warner, Jack. *My First Hundred Years in Hollywood*. NY: Random House, 1965. 331 pp. Chapter four contains references to Idora Park.

Newspapers and Periodicals:

Adams, Solly. "Miss Desmonde Celebrates." *Youngstown Vindicator* 31 May 1931: B8.

Amusement Business. 1961 to present. The weekly newspaper of the amusement park industry.

Amusement Park Journal. 1979-87.

Amusement Park Management. A trade publication published from 1928 to 1935.

"Are Barred." *Youngstown Vindicator* 10 May 1900: 3.

"Ban Lifted On Modern Dances." *Youngstown Vindicator* 16 June 1915: 3.

Bear, B.M. "Youngstown." *Motorcoach Age*. Vol. 22, #8 (August 1970).

Billboard. 1905 to 1960. A major trade weekly that covered the amusement park industry.

Carew, Dorothy M. "Youngstown Recalls Early Arc Light as Forerunner of Big Utility." *Youngstown Vindicator* 27 March 1938: L7.

Carr, Charles. "Harry G. Hamilton, Old Texas Ranger." *Youngstown Vindicator* 6 July 1920. A profile of one of Idora's founders.

Dahlinger, Charles W. "Old Allegheny." *The Western Pennsylvania Historical Magazine*, Vol. 1 (1918). An account of Allegheny's resistance to incorporation into Pittsburgh and the leading role by Grier, McAfee, and Murphy—three of Idora's founders.

Ewing, Robert M. "Charles W. Dahlinger—A Memorial." *The Western Pennsylvania Historical Magazine*, Vol. 19, #1 (March 1936): 1-4. Profile of one of Idora's founders.

"Features." *Youngstown Vindicator* 31 July 1899.

"15 Big Years Since First Car Crossed Market Street Viaduct." *Youngstown Vindicator* 31 May 1914: 1D.

"From the Horse Car To the Trolley of Today." *Youngstown Telegram* 27 November 1901: 31.

Hamilton, Esther. "Around Town." *Youngstown Vindicator* 19 June 1964:21.

"H. G. Hamilton, Capitalist and Builder, dies." *Youngstown Vindicator* 8 October 1921:1. Obituary of one of Idora's founders.

"Idora Park Is Bought By New Local Company." *Youngstown Vindicator* 3 April 1924.

"Idora Park will fold; ballroom may remain." *Youngstown Vindicator* 28 August 1984:1.

"Idora Season Opens Sunday." *Youngstown Vindicator* 22 May 1915: 5.

Jenkins, Janie S. "The Old Trolley Park." *Western Reserve Magazine* July-August 1977:10-13.

LeMonte, A. D. "Served city for 67 Years." *Youngstown Vindicator* 1 December 1940.

Madtes, George. "Idora Opens for the Season." *Youngstown Vindicator* 30 May 1920: 3D.

"Natatorium Is Acclaimed Finest in the Whole World." *Youngstown Vindicator* 13 June 1924:34.

"New Buildings and Map of Mill Creek Park." *Youngstown Vindicator* 19 March 1899.

"Pleasure Cars Meet At Frightful speed In Mid Air Sunday." *Youngstown Telegram* 24 May 1915: 1.

Roberts, Tim and Karen Guy. "Idora will Try to Open Despite $2.5 Million fire." *Youngstown Vindicator* 27 April 1984:1.

Rook, William L. "Park Psychology Based On Sex." *Youngstown Vindicator* 27 July 1930.

"Score Trapped In Cars When Dip-the-Dip Racers Collide." *Youngstown Vindicator* 24 May 1915.

Stafford, Roy. "Development of Local Street Railway System." *Youngstown Vindicator* 27 June 1911: 55.

Street Railway Journal. Major trade publication published from 1893 to 1908. Later published as *Electric Railway Journal*.

Street Railway Review. Vol. XII, No. 7, July 1902.

"A Success." *Youngstown Vindicator* 30 June 1899: 8.

"Sunday Spoke to Over Four Thousand People." *Youngstown Vindicator* 2 June 1908: 7.

Sweeney, Noreene M. "Chipping Away at a Dream." *The Carousel News & Trader* February 1994. An account of the restoration of Idora's PTC #61 carousel.

"Trolley Buses Made Way For Fleet of Today." *Youngstown Vindicator* 21 August 1988: A-8.

"Union Men." *Youngstown Vindicator* 1 August 1899: 2.

"When It's Kiddies Day at Idora." *Youngstown Vindicator* 5 July 1925:5D.

"W. H. Park Expires While on Outing in Ontario, Can." *Youngstown Telegram* 19 July 1918. Obituary of one of Idora's founders.

Youngstown Telegram 1899-1936.

Youngstown Vindicator 1893-present. (Selected articles are listed separately.)

OTHER:

Brody, Laura A. *v.* The Youngstown Park & Falls Street Railway Company and T. M. Harton, Court of Common Pleas, Mahoning County, State of Ohio. Separate Answer of T. M. Harton," 3 May 1917.

Ghosts of Idora Park (videotape). produced by WKBN TV; narrated and hosted by Laurie Jennings. 30 minute videotape sold in a limited quantity.

Idora Park (videotape). production supervised by Ed Learner. 72 minutes.

Kennywood Park, West Mifflin, PA. Company correspondence with Idora Park.

National Association of Amusement Parks and Attractions Directory and Guide. 1920-1984.

Philadelphia Toboggan Company, Philadelphia, PA. Company files and correspondence.

Rediscover Idora Park (videotape). Written by Ron Keller and Tim Young; narrated by Jim Kelly. A Kellaher, Russell, and Young Presentation. 36 minutes.

State of Ohio. *Records of Incorporation, 1893-1930*. Ohio Historical Society, Columbus, Ohio.

Youngstown State University Maag Library, Oral History Collection. Over two dozen interviews focus on Idora Park. Most helpful are the interviews with Leonard Cavalier, Alvin Conway, Stanford Csiky, Charles "Mickey" Rindin, Tillie Smedley, and John Zupko.

ACKNOWLEDGMENTS

Few books, if any, are written without the assistance of many individuals besides the authors, and *Idora Park: The Last Ride of Summer* is no exception. We are particularly grateful for the cooperation and support of Idora Park's former owners: Leonard Cavalier; Pat Duffy, Jr., his wife Marcella Duffy and daughter Kathy Duffy West; Max Rindin, and his son Mickey Rindin.

We thank the Mahoning Valley Historical Society, especially Bill Lawson, director, and Joan Reedy, assistant director, for their cooperation and permission to use many photos and documents held in the MVHS collections. A special thanks to Pam Pletcher, archivist, and former archival assistant Diane Shagla for assistance in locating documents related to Idora.

Significant information was gained from the personal recollections of the following people: Dr. Richard Murray, Mike Roncone, Dick Platt, Donald K. Hoover, Chuck Anderson, and his daughter Tammi Walsh.

Samuel High III, former president of the Philadelphia Toboggan Company, was very helpful. The successor corporation to the Philadelphia Toboggan Company, Philadelphia Toboggan Coasters, Inc., has established a wonderful archives of material from the PTC. William Dauphinee is the chief executive, Thomas Rebbie, president, and Laura Grauer, archivist.

Kennywood Park, Pittsburgh, PA, and especially Carl Hughes, chairman of the board, made available their correspondence over the years with Idora Park.

Dacia Donatella helped with much of the early research. Don Leone of City Title provided a title search that helped to clarify land ownership. Barbara Williams, archivist, and Bryan Morgan, former president, of the National Carousel Association, helped in researching Idora's Dentzel carousel and PTC #61. Captain Michael Stefko, chief arson investigator, Youngstown Fire Department, provided official reports on the 1984 and 1986 fires at Idora.

Cynthia Perantoni, Fred Dahlinger, Jr., Fred D'Amico, Charles J. Little II, Linda Little Ramage, Rain Bear Mahoney, Rev. Jason Whitehead and Rev. Mark Saunders of Mount Calvary Pentecostal Church, George Nelson, Ray Novotny, Chris Paul, and Rebecca Rogers offered information, insight, and support.

Edward C. Learner and Michael J. Brown were generous in sharing photographs from their large collections of Idora Park images.

Other significant photographs were contributed by David W. Francis, Richard Munch, and Mike Roncone. Carl Leet, Youngstown State University Media Services, provided invaluable photographic assistance.

Richard L. Bowker contributed rare postcards from his vast collection. Paul Baxley and B. Derek Shaw also provided postcards of Idora Park.

Thanks also to the following people who supplied us with photographs, documents, and other information: Doris and Bob Beck, Carol W. Bell, Cristine Campradt, Donna DeBlasio, Laurie Ann Burns Fox, Bob Fullerman, Don Hanni, Jr., Dan Kashubara, William Knecht III, Paul S. Korol and Claudia Korol, Nancy Kubina, Dan Lewis of Lewis Realty, Joan Losiewicz, Jack and Lou Ann Lovinger, Dick McKee, Dolly Billings Miller, Gail Thomas Minneman, Richard Scarsella, William Schollert, Kitty Schon, George Siessel, Mike Tarantino, Larry Walk, Tammi Walsh, WFMJ-TV, Marge Wood, and Chuck Wlodarczyk.

Some of the most historical and dramatic photographs in the book were supplied by the *Vindicator* and by Tom Molocea and Laurie Molocea of Historic Images. We are grateful for their contributions and assistance and offer a special thank you to Tony Paglia, Robert Yosay, and Sandy Deak of the *Vindicator*.

Youngstown State University provided funding through two University Research Council grants that supported much of the early research for this book.

For their endless patience and considerable research skills, we are indebted to the librarians of the Youngstown Public Library Reference Department and Periodicals Room, Youngstown State University's Maag Library, and the Pennsylvania Room of the Carnegie Library of Pittsburgh.

Karen Morrison designed the book with her usual skill and artistry. She is a joy to work with. We value her judgment and appreciate her ability to blend images and text into an attractive layout.

Betty Van Pelt Jacques encouraged the project and contributed her photographs and remembrances of the park.

Charles J. Jacques, Jr.
Rick Shale
May 1999

INDEX

(Bold, italicized page numbers refer to photographic captions.)

Aerial Joy Ride, 73
Agler, Benjamin, 46
Airplane Swing, 47, 49
Allan Herschell Company, 25
All For Fun (fun house), 42
All the Marbles, 109
Amalgamated Association of Street Railway Employees of America, 12
American Coaster Enthusiasts, 5, 107
archery, 51
Armed Forces Day, 82
Armstrong, Louis, 95
Auchy, Henry B., 28, 30, 42
auction, **120,** 120-22
Auto Skooter, 49, 76, 79, 102
Auto Speedway, 49
Avon Park, 8

Back Wabbit, 118, **119**
Baker, George J., 53
Baker, Harry, 54
Bakody, William, 26
ballroom, 22, **22-23,** 28, 56, 61, **61-63, 66, 70-71, 87, 90-91, 101,** 104, 112, 117, 124. *See also* Dancing Pavilion (1910-1984)
bandstand, 10, **15,** 64
Barge, Perry, 24
Barrel of Fun, 79
Barrett, Thomas, 46
Bartlett, Norman, 95
baseball field, 30, **47,** 54, 63, 77, **79,** 86
Baytos, Rita, 97
bear cage, **11,** 16
Bell, Boots, **95,** 95, 97
Bevin Bros. Manufacturing Company, 42
Billings, Rex, 38, **39,** 39-40, 43-47, **48,** 48-54, 98, 110
Billingsgate, **39,** 50, **108**
Biondi, Dick, 88, 92
Black Monday, 107
Blackout, 69, 79
Boeckling, George, 94
Boncilla, Sam, 77, 95
bowling alley, 12, 28
Boyle's Orchestra, 22, 25, 28, 34-35, 38, 40
Brigode, Ace, and His Fourteen Virginians, **50,** 50-51, 53
Brookdale Pony Farm, 26
Buckeye Pictures Company, 40
Buffalo Vic, 85, 95
Burns-Kasper Company, 44
Burt, Harry, 18-19
Burt's Ice Cream Stand, **16**

Cagney Brothers, 25
Calloway, Cab, **59,** 59
Camp Reynolds, 73
Carlton Brickert Players, **56,** 56
carousel, **4, 27, 30,** 34, **41,** 41-42, 49, **83,** 85, 89, **90,** 92, **93, 105,** 113, 117, **121-22,** 121-22, **126,** 126. *See also* merry-go-round
Carsonia Park, 38
Cascade Park, 24, 40, 42, 45, 49
Casino Theater, **9,** 9, 11, 17-19, 21, 24-25, **26,** 27, **29,** 29, 34-35, 60
Caterpillar, 43, **44,** 44, 78-79, **104,** 115, 126
Cathe, Leo, 56
Cavalier, Leonard A. "Tony," Jr., 78, 97-98
Cavalier, Leonard, III, 111, **117,** 119-20
Cedar Point, 26, 71, 94, 100, 102, 106
Celeron Park, 26
Central League, 58
Chance Manufacturing, 97, 100, 102, 105
Charles Browning Amusement Company, 47
Cheyenne Shootout, **104,** 104, 112-13, **114**
Cinderella's Slipper, 67
Circle Swing, 19, 23, **42,** 43, 78. *See also* Rocket Ships
Coney Island (Cincinnati, OH), 26, 52
Coney Island (New York), 22, 50, 54, 78
Conneaut Lake Park, 17, 19, 26, 45, 56, 102
Coulter, Jessie, 13-14
C. P. Huntington train, 97, **102, 114,** 115, 121
Craig Beach Park, 45
Crazy Horse Saloon, 110, 114, **119,** 124
Croslin, Joe, 77
Cunningham, Bob, 21

Dahlinger, Charles, 8-9
dancing pavilion (1899-1910; a.k.a. Casino, dancing hall), 10, **11,** 11, **18,** 59, 114
dancing pavilion (1910-1984), 22, 24, 28, 43, 48-50, 76, 87, 92. *See also* Ballroom
Dangler, 47, 49
DeAngelis, Gloria and Dolores, 74
Deibel, Charlie, **40,** 40, 44, 54, 57, **59,** 59-60, 63, 65-69, **71,** 76, **77,** 77-78, 83, 88, 98
Deibel, Victor, 78
Denehy, Daniel, 30-31
Dentzel, Gustav, 10
Dentzel carousel, 10, 24, 42. *See also* merry-go-round
Depression. *See* Great Depression
Desmonde, Lillian, 36, **40,** 40, 46, **47,** 48, **49,** 49, 54, 110.
Dietrick, Col. J. H., 19-20
Dimmick, Jimmy, 49
Dinkleman, Royal, 78
Dips. *See* Dip-the-Dips.
Dip-the-Dips, 26-27, 30-31, **32-33,** 32-33, 46
Disney, Walt, 86, 98
Disneyland, 86, 98
Dodgems, 41, 43, 79, 114

Dorney Park, 52, 97
Dragon, 62
Duffy, Pat, Jr., **2,** 2, 5, **57, 72, 87,** 104-6, 110-11, 115-16, **117,** 117, 119-120, 122
Duffy, Pat, Sr., 19, **57, 71,** 77-78, **87,** 98

Edwards, Charles, 52
Eli Bridge Company, 102
Elitch Gardens, 97
Euclid Beach Park, 19, 68, 86, 99
Evans, Billy, 57
Exposition Park, 19. *See also* Conneaut Lake Park
Eyerly Aircraft Corporation, 65-66, 103, 105

Fantasmagraph, 19
Fantastic Flying Machine, **112**
Farrar, O. R., 10, 13
Ferncliffe Park, 8
Ferris wheel, 49, 57, 69, 79, **100, 114,** 115, 120
Figure-Eight roller coaster, **16-17,** 18, **19,** 23, **26-27, 30,** 32, 35-36
fire (1951), 83
fire (1984), **2-5,** 2-5, 116, **117-18,** 117-18
fire (1986), 124
Firefly, **36,** 36, 49, 51-52
fire truck, **81,** 81
Flying Cages, **96,** 96
Flying Coaster, 95
Flying Octopus (a.k.a. Octopus), 65, **74**
Flying Scooter, 106, 112, 115
Fly-O-Plane (Flying Scooter), 106
Ford, John W., 44
Foster, Col. Lemuel T., **7,** 7, 24, 26
fun house, 41, **42,** 42-43, 47, 49, 52, 58, 65, **65-66,** 73, 76-78, **97,** 99, 103, **111,** 114, 126, 128

Geauga Lake Park, 56, 100, 102, 106
Gebruder Bruder band organ, 42
Gettins, Emily, 13-14
Giant Aeroplane Swing, 43, 49
Gilronan, Edward, 54, 56, **57,** 59
Gold Nugget, 97
Gondola Glide, 49, 67
Great Depression, 54, 56, 60, 64, 83, 94
Great Lakes Exposition, 65, **67**
Great Monkey Escape, 77-78
Grier, Samuel, 10, 14-15, 19

Hamilton, Harry G., 6-7, **9,** 9, 11-14, 20, 41
Hammond, Jack, 54
Harris, Hamilton, 8
Harton, T. M., **27,** 32, **33,** 33-34, 42, 64
Harvest Moon dances, **24,** 40
Hastings, Joseph, 9
Heidelberg Gardens, **11,** 59, **65,** 66-67, 69, 71, 76-77, 79, **83,** 88, **96,** 97, 99-100, 110, 114, **119,** 126

139

Heller, Adolph H., 44
Heller-Murray Construction Company, 45
Helter Skelter, 102, 114, 124, **127**
Hershey Park, 100
High School Day, 57, 67, 69, 71, 73
Hippodrome, 21, 43–44, 52, 54
Hively, Idora Ann, **14**, 14
Hi-Y–Tri-Hi-Y Day, 57, 67, 73, 81, 87, 101, 104
Homestead Grays, 43, 47, 54, 71
Honeymoon Trail, 73
Hooterville Highway, 100, 106, **112–13**, 115, 124
Hoover, Charles D., 23, 36, **58**, 77
Horne, Col. Frank, 23, 34
Horne Stock Company, 23, 34–36, 38, 40, 43, 46
Hot Rods, 84, 100, 115
House of David, 47
Howard, Marc, 92
Howdy Doody Show, **84**, 84–85, **94**, 95
Hrubetz, 92, 99
Huffman, Lucy, **18**, 18
Human Beingz, **98**, 99
Humpty Dump, 65
Hunt's Pier, 97

Idora Amusement Company, 2, 5, 44, 54, 67, 83
Idorables, **103, 106**, 106
Idora Dixieland Band, 100
Idora Falls, **6**, 14–15
Idora Gardens, 71, 77, 79
Idoragraph, 25
Idora Kiddy Park, 81
Idora Limited, **91, 96, 114**, 115, 126
"Idora March," **18**, 18
Idora Mill, **6**, 14
Idora Natatorium Company, 46, 67
Idora Panama Canal Company, 28
Idora Park (Oakland, California), 15
Ingersoll, Frederick, **17**, 17–18
Ingersoll Engineering & Construction Company, 17, 19
Ingersoll Pleasure Amusement Company, 19, 20, 35
Isaly's, **92**, 92–93
Ivory, Robert T., 9, 16

Jack Rabbit, 46, 49, 54, 57, 66, 77, **79**, 79, **89**, 89, 97, **99**, 104, 107, 112, **113**, 117–18, **119**, 122
James, Nellie, 22, 77
James Burtis Players, 43
Jenkins, David, 42
Jennings, Mike, 58
Jimmy Dimmick's Sunnybrook Orchestra, **46**, 48
Johnston, Hugh, 88
J. W. Zarro Company, 25

Kane, Ed, 20–21
Kasper, Edwin H., 44
KDKA, 56
Keaggy, Phil, 99
Keith and Proctor (vaudeville agency), 21, 25
Kennedy, John F., **93**, 93, 109
Kennywood Park, 17, 46, 48, 53, 56, 60, 78, 86, 100, 102, 106
Kiddie Coaster, 64, 79, **105**, 115
Kiddieland, 39, 64, 67, 69, 81, 85–86, **87**, 89, 92, 94, **96**, 96, **112, 115**, 115, **121, 123**, 126, **127**
Kiddies Day, 47, **50**, 66–67
Kings Island, 106–7
Kooky Castle, **103**, 103, 105, 114, 124, **125**, 126
Korean War, 82
Kosa, Victor, 106
Kove South, 97, **98**, 98–99, 126
Ku Klux Klan, 47

Laffin' Lena's Loonyland, **111**, 114–15, **120**, 124
lagoon, **23-24**
Lake Brady Park, 45
Lake Erie & Western Railroad, 8
Lake Shore & Michigan Southern Railroad, 8
Lake Shore Railroad, 19
Lakeside Park, 19
Lanterman, German, 26
Lanterman's Falls, **6**, 6, 14
Laughing Gallery, 18
Laughing Sal, 73
Lauterbach, E. J., 28
Leedy, Charles, 18, 60
Legros, Emile, 94
Lindy Loop, 56
Little Erie Railroad, 86
Lombardo, Guy, 59, 79–80, 95, 97, 100–101, 105
Loop-O-Plane, 64, 66
Lost River, 2, 5, 99, **100-101**, **103**, 112, 116, **116**, 118, **124**
Luna Park (Cleveland), 17
Luna Park (Coney Island, NY), 50, 54, 78
Luna Park (Pittsburgh), 17
Lush, Marion, 109, **118**, 118
Lusse, 79
Lykes Corporation, 107
Lynch, Alexander, 45

Maag, William F., Jr., **93**
Magic Carpet, 73
Mahoning & Shenango Railway and Light Company, 20–21, 24–25, 33, 36
Mahoning Valley Railway Company, 8
Mahoning Valley Street Railway, 15
Mangels, William F., 35
Market Street Viaduct, 6–7, **7, 10, 13**, 16, 19
Martin, F. M., 36
Mary-Jane Lane Stock Company, 56

McAfee, Robert, 9
McCaskey, M. E., 20
McElroys, 35–37, 40
McKelvey, L. B., 46
McSwigan, Brady, 48, 53
Melville, Frank, 19
merry-go-round (Dentzel), 8, 10, **16**. *See also* Dentzel carousel
merry-go-round (PTC #61), 57, 79. *See also* carousel
Meyers Lake Miniature Railway Company, 45
Meyers Lake Park, 56, 78, 99
Middle Atlantic League, 57–58, 68, 71, 77–78, 80, 82
mill chutes, 53
Mill Creek Park, 6, **6**, 13–14, 16, 18–19, 22, 35, 45, 77, 112
Miller, John A., 18, 42, 54, 100
Mills, Robert, 77
miniature golf, 51, 57, 97, 109, 112
Miss Teenage Youngstown, **95**, 96
Monarch Park, 19
Monkey Island, 49–50, 60, 64–65
Monroe, Vaughn, 79
Monster, 103
Montgomery, Randall, 20
Morton, Lewis, 27, 34
Morton Musical Comedy Company, 34
Morton Opera Company, 27, **34**
Motor Boat Lagoon, 79–81
Murphy, John R., 9
Murray, Thomas H., Jr., 44, 78
Myriascope, 38
Mysterious House, 20
Mysterious Knockout, 46

Nation, Carrie, 19
National Amusement Device Company, 68
Nationality Days, 61, **78**
National Register of Historic Places, 105, 113
Negro Leagues, 37, 47, 54, 71, 77
Nelson, Richard, 97
New York Railroad, 8
New York World's Fair, **71**, 73
Nixon, Richard, 89
Noble, H. D., 19
Norton, David, 121
Norton Auctioneers, 120

Oarco, 94
Octopus. *See* Flying Octopus
Ohio Edison, 36
Old Mill, **60, 64**, 64, 66, **88**, 99
1001 Troubles, 47, 49
Orbit, 94, 97
Ostanek, Walt, 118
Outdoor Dimensional Display Company, 97, 99
Over the Falls, 98

Panama Canal (ride), 27–28, 30, **31–32**, 32–33, **34**, 41, 43, 51
Panic of 1907, 20
Paragon Park, 100
Paratrooper, 99, 105, **110**, 115, **125, 128**
Park, Willis H., 6, **9**, 9, 11–12, 20, 24–25, 35
Park & Falls Street Railway Company, 6–9, **9–10**, 11, **12**, 12–14, **14**, 15–20, **21**, 22, 24, 26, 31, 33–34, 36, 41
Pay-One-Price, 99–100, 103, 106, 110
Penn-Ohio Electric Company, 36
Penn-Ohio Polka Festival, 99–101, 118, **127**
Penn-Ohio Power and Light Company, 36, 38, 40, 42, 44
Pennsylvania & Mahoning Valley Railway, 20
Pennsylvania Railroad, 8
Penny Arcade, 28, 49, 79, 86, 113–14, **115**
Philadelphia Toboggan Company (PTC), 25, 27–28, 30, 33, **34, 41**, 41–42, 51, **52**, 52–53, 73, 121
photo gallery, **15, 20**, 23, 25, **26**, 36, 38, 49, **58**
Pittsburg & Lake Erie Railroad, 8
Pittsburg & Western Railroad, 8
Platt, Royal, 24, **25**, 26, 29, 32, 36, 38, 88
pony track, 43, **61**, 76, 79
Porky the Paper-Eater, 98, **99**
Pretzel, 51–52
Princess' Visit to Youngstown, The, 32
professional wrestling, 90

Race of Nations Walkathon, 61–62, **62**
Race Through the Clouds, 33
Raisynell, 65
Rapids, 28, 51–52, **52–53, 60–61, 64**, 73, 79, 95, 99, **100**, 126
Reading Transit and Light Company, 38
R. E. Chambers Company, 64, 69, 78, 85
Record hops, 90–91
Renner, Emil, 46
Republic Railway and Light Company, 24–25, 36
Rindin, Max, **71**, 71, 78, 81, 83, 88, 95, 97–98, 100–101, 111, **117**, 119–20
Rocket Ships, 78–79, 81, 85, **89, 97, 103–4**, 114–15, **126**, 128
Rock-O-Plane, 105, **112**, 112
Rocky Springs Park, 56
Rogers, James, 74
Rogers, Volney, 8
roller skating rink, 23, 28, 32–33, 38, 40, **66**, 66, **70**, 77, 79
Roncone, Mike, **95, 98**, 98–99, 126
Roose, George, 94
Rose, George G., 21, 24
Roto-Jet, 96
Round-Up, 92
Rumpus Bumpus, 68
Ryan, Dan, 84

Schaff, Philip, 46
Schmeck, Herbert, **52**, 53–54
Scrambler, 102, 115
Sea World of Ohio, 100
Sellner Manufacturing Company, 49, 80
Send-Off Day, 71
Senior Citizen Day, 105
Shoemaker, Benjamin H., 42
Shok Shu, 64
shooting gallery, 12, 38, 79, 112
Sidesaddle, Susie, 91–93
Skee Ball, 47, 49, 112
Skydiver, 100
Sky King, **92**, 93
Skywheel, 89
Smith, Buffalo Bob, **84**, 85, 95
Smith, George P., Jr., 53
Smith, H. S., 42
Smith, Vic. *See* Buffalo Vic
Sourbeck, Frank, 18–19
Sousa, John Philip, **35**, 35
South Side Land & Improvement Company, 11, 20
Spider, 105, **112**, 112, 120
Spillman Engineering Company, 57
Springbrook Park Company, 45
Squaw Creek Park, 8
Stanley, Edward, 9, 11–12, 14, 18–19, **19**, 59–60
Stock, Bert, 60
Stratoship, 64
Sullivan, John L., 21
Summit Beach Park, 56
Sunday, Billy, 21
Sweeney, Frank, 95
swimming pool, **45**, 45–46, **48**, 49, **58**, 58, 66, 73–75, **75**, 79, **80**, 86, 115

Tarona Players, **45**, 54
Terminal Park, 8, 11–13
theater, 8, **9**, 10, 12, **13**, 15, 27, **29**, 39, 48–49, 54, 59
Thunderbolt (Kennywood), 100
Tilt-A-Whirl, 49, 80, **101–2**, 104, 115
Tin Can Party, 72
T. M. Harton Company, 25–27, 31–33, 46
Toboggan Amusement Company, 33–34
Tod, Henry, 8
To Helenback, 58
Trabant, 97
Tracey, Bill, 97, 99
Traver, Harry, 23, 43
Traver Engineering Company, 44, 64
Trigg, Winter, **20**, 22
Trimpers, 97
Truman, Harry S., 96–97
Tumble Bug, 69
Turbo, 102
Turney, Doris, 98
Turtle, 74, 85, 112

Vettel, Edward, 46, 64

Wade, Angus S., 22
Walbridge Park, 26
Waldameer Park, 19, 78
Walentas, David and Jane, 122
Walk, Larry, 99, 109, **118**
Walsh, Tammi, 98
Walt Disney World, 98
Warner, Jack, 16
Warner Brothers, 16, 38
water rifle range, 38
WBBW, 84, 88
Weiss, Gustav, 42
West View Park, 26, 56, 64, **74–75**, 106
WFMJ, **84**, 84, 87, **91–92**, 92–93
Whacky Shack, 99, 114
Whip, 35, 47, 49, 68, 79, 85
WHOT, 88, 101, 104–6, 118
Wildcat, **3**, 4, **5**, 5, **51–55**, 51–54, 57, 59, **61**, 66, 68, 77–79, **82–83**, 85, 85, 99–100, **105**, 105, **107**, 107, **110–11**, 113, **116**, 116–18, **122**, 122, **126**, 126, **128**
Wilde Maus (Wild Mouse), 96
William Dentzel Company, 25
Willis Park (athletic field), 35
Wizard of Oz (ride), 43, 49, 51
WKBN, 60, 62
Women's Christian Temperance Union, 58
Wood, Ethel and Bob, 81
Woodland Beach Park, 19
World War II, 69, 71–72, **73**, 75, 83, 94, 100
Wright Field, 34

Yankovic, Frankie, 118
Young, Cy, 82
Youngstown Athletics, 80–83
Youngstown Browns, 68–69, **69**, 71
Youngstown Buckeyes, 57–58
Youngstown Carrousel Company, 42, 49
Youngstown College, 82
    See also Youngstown University
Youngstown Colts, 77–78, 80
Youngstown Consolidated Gas & Electric Company, 19–20
Youngstown Gremlins, 77, **78**
Youngstown Military Band, 10, 72
Youngstown Municipal Railway, 36
Youngstown Oaklands, 50
Youngstown Park & Falls Street Railway Company. *See* Park & Falls Street Railway Company
Youngstown-Sharon Railway and Light Company, 20
Youngstown Sheet and Tube Company, 63, 68, **68**, 72, 107–8
Youngstown University, 87, **90–91**, 95, **96**, 97 *See also* Youngstown College
Youth On Parade, **67**, 84
Yo-Yo, 105, 112

BOOKS FROM AMUSEMENT PARK JOURNAL

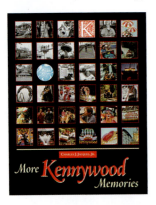

MORE KENNYWOOD MEMORIES by Charles J. Jacques, Jr. is a companion book to his first Kennywood book *(Kennywood: Roller Coaster Capital of the World)*. This new book does not replace the first book because not one of the images or illustrations used in the first book appears in the second. At the back of the 224-page book is a large appendix of facts about Kennywood Park from its founding in 1898 to its one hundredth season. The book covers the early years, the Laser Loop, Steel Phantom, Raging Rapids, Lost Kennywood, the rebuilt Noah's Ark, and the Pitt Fall. In addition, there are chapters on Kennywood's two sister parks, Idlewild and Sandcastle. There are 642 images with 105 of them in color. Size 8 1/2 x 11 inches.

This softcover book is available for $29.95, shipping and handling included.

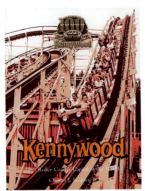

KENNYWOOD: ROLLER COASTER CAPITAL OF THE WORLD by Charles J. Jacques, Jr. This 212-page book was first published in 1982. The book has gone through six printings and has sold more than 23,000 copies. There are 450 photographs and other images that are not duplicated in Jacques' second Kennywood book *More Kennywood Memories*. Kennywood coasters from the 1902 Figure Eight to the Laser Loop are covered as are many other attractions such as Noah's Ark, Dentzel Carousel, circle swing, and funhouses. Size 8 1/2 x 11 inches.

This softcover book is available for $24.95, shipping and handling included.

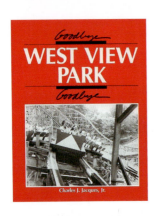

GOODBYE, WEST VIEW PARK, GOODBYE by Charles J. Jacques, Jr., a history of one of Pittsburgh's amusement parks from its founding by T. M. Harton in 1906 until it was closed after the 1977 season. Included in this 124-page book are many photographs of West View Park's terrific roller coasters, the Kiddie Dips, the Dips and Racing Whippet, designed by the Vettel family. Rare photographs of the carousel built by Harton with horses carved by the Muller brothers of Philadelphia, and West View Park's famous Danceland which played all of the major dance bands over the years. Size 8 1/2 x 11 inches.

This softcover book is available for $24.95, shipping and handling included.

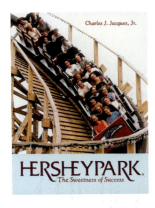

HERSHEYPARK: THE SWEETNESS OF SUCCESS by Charles J. Jacques, Jr. was published in 1997. The 224-page book tells the story of Hershey Park from its founding in 1907 by chocolate magnate Milton S. Hershey to the 1997 season. Hersheypark's roller coasters such as the Wildcat, Comet, and sooperdooper Looper and carousels along with the swimming pool, Kiddieland, the Whoops, TIDAL FORCE, and the Kissing Tower are included. The book has 483 photographs (36 in color). Size 8 1/2 x 11 inches.

This book is available at $19.95 for the softcover and $29.95 for the hardcover, shipping and handling included.

Printed in U.S.A.
General Press Corporation
Natrona Heights, PA 15065

P.O. Box 478 • Jefferson, OH 44047-0478
(440) 576-6531   Fax: (440) 576-5850
Email: apjacqu@suite224.net